"Lorsch and Tierney have finally written, if not the last word, certainly the most definitive word, on professional service firms. There is nothing out there that comes close to catching the nuance, the complexity, and the subtlety of these important institutions and how they are led and managed. *Aligning the Stars* is a home run."

—Warren Bennis, Distinguished Professor of Business, University of Southern California, and author of *Managing the Dream*

"The stars of the title are those exceptionally talented people on whom successful businesses increasingly depend. The word is well chosen. Stars can be vain, greedy, insecure, and infinitely time-consuming. But they remain indispensable: Companies without stars will never come in better than second. This invaluable work gives comprehensive guidance on their care and maintenance: how to find, attract, motivate, and reward. A handbook for winners."

—Sir Martin Sorrell, Chief Executive Officer, WPP Group PLC

"With clear principles and many stimulating examples, this well-written book will provoke reflection and debate among professional firm leaders."

—David H. Maister, coauthor of *First Among Equals*

"Revenues for professional service firms have mushroomed nearly ten times in the past twenty years, and they now hire over 60 percent of the M.B.A.s from top schools. Finally, we have a first-rate book that explains the secrets of the very best of these firms—how they almost magically align their stars and their strategies, building trust as they build their own futures. Jay Lorsch and Tom Tierney are sometimes iconoclastic, often provocative, and always, always informative."

—David Gergen, Director, Center for Public Leadership, John F. Kennedy School of Government, Harvard University

ALIGNING THE STARS

JAY W. LORSCH ★ THOMAS J. TIERNEY

ALIGNING THE STARS

HOW TO SUCCEED WHEN PROFESSIONALS DRIVE RESULTS

HARVARD BUSINESS SCHOOL PRESS

Boston, Massachusetts

978-1-57851-513-4 (ISBN 13)

Printed in the United States of America

11 10 09 08 07   6 7 8 9 10

Requests for permission to use or reproduce material from this book should be directed to permissions@hbsp.harvard.edu, or mailed to Permissions, Harvard Business School Publishing, 60 Harvard Way, Boston, Massachusetts 02163.

Library of Congress Cataloging-in-Publication Data
Lorsch, Jay William.
    Aligning the stars : how to succeed when professionals drive results/ Jay W. Lorsch, Thomas J. Tierney.
        p. cm.
    Includes index.
    ISBN 1-57851-513-0 (alk. paper)
        1. Professional corporations—Management. I. Tierney, Thomas J., 1954–
II. Title.

HD62.65.L67 2002
658–dc21

2001051535

To Nina and Teá, two future stars!
J. W. L.

To my wife Karen, and our sons
Colin and Braden
T. J. T.

Contents

Acknowledgments

The discussions, research, and writing that created this book spanned almost five years. During that time, many organizations and individuals provided the resources and effort that led to the results you will find in the following pages. We are extremely grateful for this support, insight, and encouragement.

First, we wish to thank the leaders and professionals in the eighteen outstanding professional service firms that were the focus of our research. They were generous with their time, experience, and insights. We also wish to acknowledge the contribution of the executives of the first-generation technology consulting firms that we studied. Their cooperation occurred in the midst of an extremely challenging period in their history. We learned a great deal from all these talented professionals!

We also wish to express our gratitude to the two organizations that supported this effort financially: Bain & Company and the Division of Research of the Harvard Business School. Their support enabled us to complete the actual research and provided the flexibility for us to collaborate and write this book.

Numerous colleagues at Bain & Company and Harvard Business School were a source of knowledge and inspiration to us both. In multiple conversations, they provided ideas that found their way into these pages. We especially want to recognize several of Tom's colleagues at Bain, including John Donahoe, Wendy Miller, Katie Smith-Milway, Fred Reichheld, Phyllis Yale, and Chris Zook, who read and reacted to various drafts, provided informal advice, and helped advance our thinking. At HBS, Paul Lawrence provided similar wise counsel.

Other important contributors included Jeff Bradach, Bob Buford, and Maryann Hedaa. A special thanks is due Jim Collins, whose experience and wisdom helped shape our final manuscript.

We also wish to thank the participants and faculty of the Leading Professional Services Firms Executive Education program at Harvard Business School, especially Tom DeLong, Jack Gabarro, and Ashish Nanda. Many of the ideas, particularly the concept of alignment, were tested and refined in interactions with them.

During the course of our investigations, several researchers assisted us in collecting and analyzing enormous amounts of data. At Bain we wish to thank Claire Alexander, Charu Chandrasekhar, Tamar Dor-Ner, Jason Jennings, Neil Kalvelage, Jodi Walsh, and Steve Wunker. At Harvard, we are indebted to Dan Erickson (who worked tirelessly on the project for two years), Lisa Haueisen Rohrer, and Sara Hindels.

Even with the advent of word processing technology, books do not appear without the dedicated and competent support of assistants. We are extremely grateful to Jane Barrett at the Harvard Business School, and Jennifer Judge, Linda Polmear, Ann Stapleton, and Bryan Teixeira at Bain & Company. It was they who coordinated the numerous meetings and made sure that the countless drafts were accurate and complete.

Nor can books appear without the support of experienced publishing professionals. We are grateful to Amanda Elkin, Carol Franco, and Melinda Merino of the Harvard Business School Press.

Finally, we wish to recognize three contributors in particular, who became an integral part of what came to be known as "The Book Club": Katharina Pick, Nan Stone, and Regina Maruca. As a research associate at Harvard Business School for three years, Kat helped complete the field research, then led the analysis and organization of these data, and finally ended up providing editorial assistance. When it came to creating a title for the book, her suggestion, "Aligning the Stars," prevailed!

Nan and her colleague, Regina, were the editorial and literary glue that held us, and the book, together. Nan's skilled and insightful advice, her flair with words, and her editorial wisdom synthesized our two voices and sharpened our thinking. Regina's support and commitment similarly helped us improve each and every chapter.

The process of developing and writing this book has been something of a shared adventure. Every participant has played a role in a meaningful way over months or years to help produce our final product. The experience was challenging and exhilarating for us all. We are extremely grateful to everyone who contributed, and hope they take pride in our joint creation.

Boston, MA
December 5, 2001

ALIGNING THE STARS

1 ★ Introduction

A Reader's Guide

EVERYONE knows the old adage, "those who can, do; those who can't, teach." But suppose a doer and a teacher got together around a shared passion. What would happen? We tried this experiment, and *Aligning the Stars* is the result.

Tom is a practitioner who brings a "what do we do Monday morning" perspective to the management and leadership of professional firms. Jay is a Harvard Business School professor who has been studying and writing about organizational behavior for almost forty years. We first met in the context of the one-week Executive Education program, Leadership in Professional Service Firms, which Jay teaches at HBS. One of the cases focused on the challenges that Bain & Company, the management-consulting firm, faced in the late 1980s. As

Bain's chief executive, Tom spoke at the session devoted to the case. Afterward we continued to meet and talk. Soon we found ourselves engaged in a joint project designed to help us understand why some professional service firms (PSFs) succeeded through the ups and downs of business cycles, while others—seemingly similar—drifted and fell behind.

This book attempts to answer that question in a way that will be useful to professionals and their organizations. The lawyers who aggressively advocate their client's interests. The advertising agency executives who help build brands. The executive search firms who help place CEOs. The technology service providers and engineers who create and sustain information systems (and influence over 50 percent of capital expenditures in business today). The strategy consultants who help chart the future for their clients. The human resources experts who assist their clients with "change management" while managing the retirement programs for their clients' employees. The accountants who conduct audits and provide tax advice. The investment bankers who in 2000 facilitated a record $1.7 trillion of M&A transactions. The specialists who advise on decisions ranging from public relations and product design to real estate and product distribution.

The book's title reveals our bottom line: Outstanding firms are consistently able to identify, attract, and retain star performers; to get stars committed to their firm's strategy; to manage stars across geographic distance, business lines, and generations; to govern and lead so that both the organization and its stars prosper and feel rewarded. These capabilities are what give great firms their competitive advantage. Together, they constitute the work of aligning the stars.

In the pages that follow, you will see what this requires and how it can be accomplished. For now, two definitions are in order. First is what we mean by stars.

As we use the term, *stars* are the men and women in critical jobs whose performance is crucial to their organization's success. In PSFs their ranks include younger professionals as well as seasoned executives; and their titles—such as managing director, vice president, and partner—are as various as their organizations. What stars have in common is not only a record of past accomplishments but also, and more important, the potential to continue contributing to their firm's success. This means that they are also the individuals who have the highest future value to their organization. How much of this value is realized—or whether it is realized at all—ultimately depends on the degree of alignment between the stars and their organization.

Alignment means creating organizational practices and structures that simultaneously fit the strategic requirements of a business and the needs of its key employees. Academics and consultants have been familiar with the concept for decades, and field research (including ours) has demonstrated its contribution to organizational success many times over.[1] Moreover, it is intuitively appealing: It makes sense that the more the people in a company are motivated to perform in ways that achieve the company's goals, the greater the likelihood that the company will succeed. Yet despite alignment's familiarity and common-sense appeal, for many businesspeople the concept remains just that, a concept. However useful and important alignment may appear, it just isn't something managers talk about—let alone explicitly "do"—on Monday morning.

Yet great enduring firms *are* aligned. Their organization and strategy are mutually reinforcing; individuals work to advance the best interests of the firm. Aligned companies enjoy competitive success and financial strength; they become industry leaders. Although their managers may not discuss alignment, they do *think* alignment; the consequence of their cumulative decisions and behaviors is an aligned organization.

Alignment is much easier to conceptualize, and to describe after the fact, than it is to create. Achieving alignment involves understanding that your organization is a system in which every decision influences—and is influenced by—every other decision, and then making choices that will reinforce its strategy and values. Sometimes the connections are simple and straightforward. A decision about what criteria to use as the basis for your firm's compensation plan, for example, will clearly affect how the professionals divide their time between serving existing clients and developing new ones. In such instances it's easy to see why and how one decision relates to—and must be integrated with—another (in this case, the firm's strategy).

Often, however, the relationships are not so transparent or immediate. For example, we know of one firm, worried about employee retention, that penalized its partners financially for professional turnover. Turnover dropped to near zero—but so did the quality of the firm's work because mediocre performers were retained and even promoted. If alignment is to be created and maintained, unintended consequences like these also need to be considered and worked through. By and large, this is not a comfortable way for the human mind to work. Most of us prefer to think and discuss things in a linear fashion, and to link cause and effect one decision at a time. The fact that real-life decisions and choices usually present themselves not as pieces of an integrated whole but on a one-off basis only reinforces this preference.

Alignment is also hard to achieve because the environment in which organizations compete and serve customers is constantly changing. New services and competitive approaches can require changes in organization. Furthermore, alignment often requires people to make changes that will advance the organization's well-being at their own expense. For these reasons, alignment is always a work in progress, with organizations slipping out of alignment as client needs, competitive activities, and leaders change, and as individual interests prevail.

Nevertheless, alignment is essential—and never more so than in times of business turbulence like those PSFs are now experiencing. Even for the best and most long-lived professional firms, success in the decades ahead will rest on whether the majority of their accomplished professionals perform at their full potential, in a manner that meets the needs of the firm.

Our Approach

The jumping-off point for *Aligning the Stars* was the research project we began in 1997, which focused on uncovering the strategic and organizational practices of successful PSFs. First, we defined *professional service firms* as those that provide professional assistance to the business community; that is, accounting firms, advertising agencies, management consultants, executive search firms, investment banks, information technology consulting firms, and, most numerous of all, law firms. Next we addressed the question of how to define success. Financial performance was one criterion: to qualify for inclusion in the study, PSFs had to be profitable and growing. Reputation was another criterion: we wanted to choose firms that were respected by their peers as well as those outside their profession. Finally, we sought firms that had stood the test of time in two respects: they had weathered business cycles, demonstrating the ability to survive downturns as well as ride the waves of economic expansion; and they had evolved well beyond their founding generation.

On the basis of these criteria we identified eighteen U.S.-based firms that were widely considered to be among the leaders in their field. In three cases, Price Waterhouse, Alex Brown, and Goldman Sachs, their roots went back to the nineteenth century. Several more were founded well before the Second World War: Ernst & Young, Grey Advertising, Fulbright & Jaworski, Latham & Watkins, and McKinsey. Last but not least were the "newcomers": Ogilvy & Mather, Young & Rubicam, Korn/Ferry, Heidrick & Struggles, Hambrecht & Quist, American Management Systems, IBM Consulting, Skadden Arps, Wachtell, Lipton, and Bain. (For a list of these firms by business, see the appendix at the end of this book.) In addition to reviewing publicly available data, we spoke with senior leaders at each of these firms to understand how they thought about its strategy, organization, and culture. Unless otherwise noted in the text, all quotations in the book come from these interviews.

Even as we studied these firms, however, the pace of change in the sector was accelerating. Since we began our work in 1997, almost every firm has changed, reflecting the dynamics of the marketplace. Consider just the three "old-timers." Price Waterhouse merged with Coopers & Lybrand to become PricewaterhouseCoopers. Alex Brown was acquired by Bankers Trust, which was acquired in turn by Deutsche Banc. Goldman Sachs, which has helped so many other companies go public, decided to go public itself.

Adding to the turmoil were the dot-com start-ups. Their business models, organizational approaches, and stunning (though short-lived) commercial success piqued our interest. Despite the subsequent decline in their economic fortunes, we knew that there would be lessons to learn from their experiences. So we delved into the wealth of public information and also interviewed executives from half-a-dozen of the more prominent pioneers: Cysive, Diamond Cluster, Digitas, Sapient, Scient, and Viant.

To achieve success you must understand failure. Ultimately, we broadened our research agenda to include firms (old and new) that seemed to have lost their bearings. What happened to Cambridge Technology Partners? Why did CSC Index disappear? Where did Mitchell Madison, U.S. Web, and, subsequently, March First all go wrong? Why has A.D. Little, the oldest consulting firm, had so many serious problems? In total we gathered public data on another fifty firms, including high-profile debacles such as Shearson-Lehman, Saatchi & Saatchi, and Gaston & Snow.

We cannot tell all the stories on these limited pages, but we strive to convey the lessons—the "So what?"—in a manner we hope you will find useful. Our goal is to be both conceptual and practical, to focus on the handful of levers that are critical in leading a prosperous professional service firm. There is enormous similarity across the various businesses encompassed within professional services. Your organization's challenges are not as unique as you might believe. Law firms can learn from consulting firms. Ad agencies can learn from law firms. Information technology firms can learn from executive search firms, and so on. While the businesses are different, the business models are strikingly similar. They all rely on selling high-priced time and services on a sustainable basis, and that, in turn, depends on building client relationships and delivering client value—value that cannot easily be measured and often relies heavily on clients' perceptions.

From Ideas to Practice

While many professional service firms (and the sector overall) have never been stronger, they also have never been more challenged. Traditional business boundaries are dissolving, ushering in new competitive threats. Questions about globalization, technology, ownership, and scale abound. Some firms have grown so large and diversified, for instance, that they are adopting corporate-like approaches, which may not suit the inherent nature of their businesses. For better and worse, PSFs are entering uncharted territory, as chapter 2 makes clear.

Because people's behavior is influenced by myriad variables, many of which also influence one another, alignment is a systems challenge. It cannot be achieved by obsessing over any single dimension of the business. Nevertheless, the temptation to do so can be enormous. Think about all the time and attention many firms devote to strategic plans that are never implemented. Or the energy expended on creating performance review systems designed to motivate certain kinds of behavior that ultimately fall flat.

In PSFs, alignment is a consequence of two separate but interdependent phenomena: the choices the firm's leadership make over time on a handful of critical dimensions and the behaviors of the professionals who implement those choices day by day. Practically speaking, this means that four aspects of the firm are central to the work of creating alignment: strategy, organization (which includes people systems as well as structure and governance), culture, and leadership.

Effective strategy hinges on serving specific clients' needs better than your competitors. In PSFs, that means making coherent and fact-based decisions about your target clients and your value proposition to those clients vis-à-vis competition. This incorporates decisions about geographic strategy, pricing strategy, and business-line strategy, among others. These decisions cannot be divorced from one another, and they must not be based on wishful thinking or yesterday's reality. Strategy is discussed in chapter 3.

In the realm of organization, a handful of choices matter most. People systems—which encompass recruitment, deployment, performance management, and compensation—form the firm's human resource backbone. In chapter 4 we look at how outstanding firms design their people systems to meet the challenge of turning talented newcomers into stars. Then we turn to a more complex challenge: developing and motivating accomplished stars—the partner-level professionals who are the firm's managers and owners as well as its chief revenue producers. How the firm's people systems can influence these independent-minded professionals to act as leaders within the firm is the subject of chapter 5.

Two other facets of the organization—structure and governance—have a huge impact on whether a firm is aligned. The organization's *structure* clarifies who does what and who reports to whom. *Governance* refers to how decisions get made and who gets to make them. These organizational dimensions, which are deeply rooted in the principle of partnership, are the topic of chapter 6.

Culture is central to shaping behavior (and thus sustaining alignment) and to attracting and retaining stars. Contrary to popular belief, we believe that culture is not a given—that it both can and must be managed. Chapter 7 discusses how.

Finally, alignment cannot exist without effective leadership. In PSFs, every partner's day-to-day behavior matters because each of them can exert personal leadership, even if they do not all have formal management responsibilities. For this reason, the importance of personal leadership weaves throughout the book. Leadership, however, is also the exclusive topic of chapter 8, which focuses on those partners who assume formal leadership positions (such as CEOs) as well as office heads, practice leaders, and functional leaders. These people are ultimately accountable for aligning the stars, yet they usually lack the power and control associated with similar positions in a typical corporate setting. They hold some of the most important and challenging leadership positions in business today.

In chapter 9, our book turns to a more personal focus. Because PSFs depend on outstanding professionals, the personal needs, motivation, and careers of individuals (young and old) are of utmost importance. This is, indeed, the essence of a people business—and the people in these businesses are confronting more challenges and choices than ever before. This chapter is especially for you, our reader: Whether you are a partner-level executive or an aspiring young associate, a professional who is immersed in serving clients or one charged with significant management responsibilities, we think you will find it thought-provoking and personally relevant.

Albert Einstein is reported to have said, "Questions are more important than answers." We agree. No book can offer its readers customized answers to all the particular decisions they and their organizations face. But good books can prompt their readers to *pursue* the *few* questions that really matter. Ultimately, success depends on saying *no* to pressing but inconsequential questions, while concentrating your energy on those few questions that will determine your firm's destiny and your own. We hope this book will help you and your colleagues ask—and answer—those critical questions.

2 ★ Impact and Influence

The World of Professional Services

IT WOULD be hard to discover a significant company in today's tumultuous business environment that does not rely heavily on some mix of professional services. From the boardroom to the shop floor, the footprints of professionals are everywhere. Boards of directors and CEOs work with strategy consultants, investment bankers, lawyers, and executive search firms. Marketing departments engage advertising agencies. The chief technology officer employs an army of information technology providers. Human resources, manufacturing, sales—they too rely on outside professionals.

Sometimes professionals work on make-or-break corporate decisions like whether to initiate an antitrust lawsuit or acquire a major new business. In other instances, their assignments are more tactical, to redesign a compensation program, for instance, or to improve manufacturing throughput. In all these situations, clients pay professionals handsomely for their advice and expertise. They trust these outsiders to help them make complex decisions and implement important initiatives.

As long as respect and trust are maintained between professional and client, it is natural for the client to directionally follow the advisor's recommendations. The iterative, consensus-building process between professional and client becomes the foundation for repeat business and the basis for an ongoing commercial relationship. Professionals' expertise vis-à-vis their clients means that professional service firms (PSFs) exert enormous influence—an influence that at times helps shape the destiny of the clients they serve.

Clients, primarily the so-called Fortune 1000, are demanding more and more professional services. As shown in figure 2-1, global revenue for professional services climbed steadily from 1980 to 2000. In 1980, professional services generated $107 billion in revenue. By

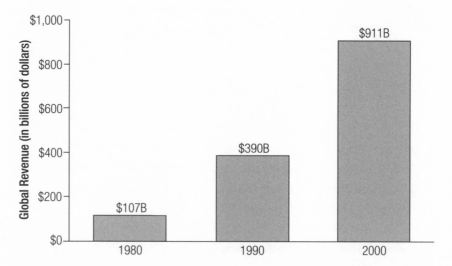

Source: IDC "Worldwide Consulting Forecasts," 1995–2002, 1997–2004; Kennedy Information Group; SDC database; American Lawyer; Advertising Age; Accounting Today: U.S. Industry and Trade Outlook; Business Insurance; US Market Trends & Forecasts; Euromonitor; Salomon Smith Barney.

Figure 2-1　**Global Revenue for Professional Services, 1980–2000**

1990, that had increased over 300 percent to $390 billion. By 2000, total professional service revenue had grown to just short of a trillion dollars. That translates into an 11 percent compound annual growth rate for professional services from 1980 to 2000, during which American gross national product (GNP) grew at 3.7 percent and manufacturing activities grew at 4.6 percent. Many established professional firms saw their revenue increase two and a half, even ten times during the recent decade.[1]

Demand for professional services is fueling the emergence of new industries: Today we take the ten-billion-dollar executive search business for granted, yet it only emerged in the late 1970s. Similarly, the Internet phenomenon generated hundreds of new Web-focused consulting firms, as well as massive expansion within established firms such as Accenture (formerly Andersen Consulting) and American Management Systems.

Professional services have become so financially attractive and strategically important that traditional companies are also entering and expanding within the sector. Hewlett-Packard attempted (and failed) to purchase PricewaterhouseCoopers's consulting business; the company's quest to strengthen its service business is now a central part of its rationale for its proposed acquisition of Compaq. The same rationale caused EDS to acquire the consulting firm A.T. Kearney in 1998. IBM generated almost 40 percent of its 2000 revenue from its Global Services unit (including outsourcing), which only began in the late 1980s.

Even the public capital markets are becoming enamored with professional services. After a decade of debate, Goldman Sachs went public in 1999. Leading executive search firms including Korn/Ferry and Heidrick & Struggles did likewise. For a while, so-called new economy consulting firms were the darlings of Wall Street.

Despite the emergence of a few publicly traded PSFs, however, the size and scope of the sector remains largely invisible to most businesspeople. Clients are aware of the firms—and particularly the individuals within those firms—with whom they interact. But the sector itself is a hidden giant. Like an iceberg whose mass lies mostly beneath the sea, much of this dynamic sector is unseen and unexplored.

Why? One reason is the behavior of professionals themselves. Whether lawyers or accountants, management consultants or advertising executives, professionals all tend to work mostly in the wings while their clients occupy center stage. Wisdom, not modesty, dictates this behavior. Professionals succeed by helping their clients succeed, by maintaining strong confidential relationships, by giving rather than taking credit. One consequence of this behavior is that relatively little has been written about professional service firms: how they succeed, how they fail, and what they might have to teach other companies about competing in businesses in which talented people are the source of competitive advantage. In addition, for decades, PSFs were privately held and managed for the benefit of their partner–owners (as many still are, and as U.S. law and accounting firms are required by law to be). They competed in relatively fragmented industries with hundreds, even thousands, of overlapping providers. Wall Street analysts did not follow them. Reporters did not write about them. Authors of best-selling business books like *In Search of Excellence* (1982) and *Built to Last* (1995) that chronicled the behaviors of outstanding companies avoided professional service firms.

Nor did business educators focus on professional services. Harvard Business School's executive education programs, which began in 1943, were the first of their kind; the school's first course on professional services was not offered until the mid-1990s. For decades, David Maister was the only widely known academic/practitioner who focused on this powerful and diverse sector.[2]

The lack of attention is all the more striking when you consider that 65 percent of the M.B.A.s from top graduate business schools begin their careers in professional services. This compares with less than 20 percent who enter manufacturing. At Stanford Business School, companies such as Intel, Dell Computer, and Circuit City Stores have stopped recruiting altogether, in part because of their inability to compete with consulting, investment banking, and private equity firms. (Similar challenges have long confronted corporations seeking to hire the best young lawyers and accountants.)

The best and brightest graduates know what they are doing. Starting compensation in professional services is higher than the average of all other job opportunities. These people can expect to work with exceptionally bright colleagues on interesting problems. Professional development and training are typically superb. Furthermore, a few years in a top PSF will likely accelerate their careers long-term, as a stepping-stone to an outstanding opportunity in a client organization, for instance, or possibly to a leadership role in an attractive start-up venture. In short, these graduates are being rational. The competitive marketplace for top business talent is speaking: Corporations face a challenge competing effectively for talent against their professional service providers.

At least in the short run. What do executives like Lou Gerstner (CEO of IBM), Ken Chenault (CEO of American Express), Meg Whitman (CEO of eBay), Herb Kelleher (CEO of Southwest Airlines), and Charles Conaway (Chairman and CEO of Kmart) have in common? All are alumni of professional service firms. These firms may be the single greatest source of top talent in U.S. business today. Given their aggregate scale and the reality of a 10 to 20 percent annual turnover, these firms are becoming the finishing schools for more and more aspiring top executives.

In addition to talent, PSFs are increasingly supplying capital to other industries. Private equity and venture capital firms invested $91 billion in 2000, up from $32 billion in 1990. Bain & Company launched its investment vehicle, Bain Capital, in 1985; by 2000, McKinsey, PricewaterhouseCoopers, Heidrick & Struggles, and Accenture (to name just a few) had followed suit. Investment banks such as Hambrecht & Quist and Goldman Sachs have been both service providers and principals for years. (Law firms such as Wilson, Sonsini, the Venture Law Group, and O'Melveny & Myers have also begun to play both roles.) If you examine the biographies of the men and women who guide the investment of private money into start-ups, turn-arounds, and leveraged buyouts, you will often find alumni of investment banks, law firms, and consulting firms.

Last but not least, PSFs are becoming knowledge engines for business. The number of business books doubled during the 1990s, with professionals rivaling (if not outpacing) academics among the ranks of authors.[3] Professionals publish books, write articles, distribute electronic newsletters, and host conferences. Increasingly they are an important source of innovative services and ideas.

Are professionals and their firms taking over the business world? Of course not. But they may be the most powerful and unexplored source of value (both direct and indirect) in modern business. As direct service providers and as sources of talent, capital, and knowledge, their global impact is exceptional.

The expansion of PSF impact will likely extend into the twenty-first century. Peter Drucker, the renowned management guru, has long argued that the decades ahead belong to "knowledge workers." "International economic theory is obsolete," he told *Wired* magazine back in 1993. "The traditional factors of production—land, labor, and capital—are becoming restraints rather than driving forces. Knowledge is becoming the one critical factor of production."[4] And in situation after situation he is being proved correct. The belief that competitive advantage will increasingly depend on intangibles such as knowledge and expertise rather than tangibles such as plant and equipment is widespread. Certainly the economics of knowledge-based products like software eventually overwhelm the commodity-like margins of hardware. In consumer goods, top brands earn profit premiums independent of their manufacturing and distribution costs because of intangible *brand value*. The commercialization of the Internet is also opening countless new profit opportunities in which ideas prevail over things.

A Mutually Dependent Relationship

In the industries fueling the economic growth of developed countries around the globe, corporate profits will be increasingly dependent on the value knowledge workers create. But who will employ these talented individuals? The evidence suggests that the knowledge and expertise embedded in broadly defined "professional services" will increasingly be outsourced: More and more corporations will logically decide to buy from others what they are unable to make themselves at a similar price and quality. Law firms already provide the vast majority of legal services despite the existence of corporate legal staffs. Planning departments hire consultants to augment their internal capabilities.

Marketing organizations employ ad agencies because they know that the agencies possess expertise different from their own.

Corporations are now purchasing brainpower from suppliers the way they have long been accustomed to purchasing raw materials and parts. At one time, for example, auto manufacturers produced all their own parts. Not today. Like many industrial companies, they eventually concluded that backward integration was costly and ineffective. Now the same kind of thinking is being applied to professional services. Why backward integrate into a very different business when outstanding providers can meet your needs better and more effectively? Especially when it's a challenge to recruit and retain professionals—and when internal demand for their services is episodic and somewhat unpredictable.

This practical reality has two related consequences. One, clearly evident already, is that PSFs of all sorts are gaining scale. The other is that the client corporations' success will depend heavily upon the firms they hire and the quality of the services those firms' professionals provide. The more important an economic factor knowledge becomes, the more PSFs will shape competitive advantage (or disadvantage) for their clients. In aggregate, the quality of their work will drive their clients' success.

This simple thought has significant ramifications because it is exceptionally difficult to measure the quality of professional services, much less the actual value they add. In many client relationships, the professionals work so closely with their client counterparts that it's hard to say at the end of the day who did what, client or service provider. The inherently intangible nature of professional services makes comparing suppliers even more challenging. And as any sophisticated buyer of professional services knows, it's not the firm that matters most, but the specific individuals who work on the project. They will drive the value added.

Given this, it is crucial that buyers of professional services understand how PSFs work and what distinguishes great firms from good (and less good) competitors. Experienced executives, who rely on a vast array of professionals and firms to meet their needs, are increasingly aware of the impact these professionals can have on their futures.

In the years ahead, no one in business will be able to ignore the looming iceberg that is the professional service sector.

The PSF Business Model

The professional service sector is grounded in a unique business model, which is centered on productively managing highly paid professionals. The best firms excel at this, not just in the short term but over decades and across business cycles. As a result, their experience offers valuable lessons for newer (or less adroit) professional firms as well as for any business that must attract, retain, and motivate talented individuals.

Whether a firm is a worldwide organization with hundreds of partners or a sole proprietorship, the basic building block of its business model is the client relationship (see figure 2-2). Let's start with the simplest example, a single professional selling his services to a single customer. (This could be your personal financial advisor, lawyer, or accountant.) What are you buying? At one level, you're purchasing time, but mostly you're concerned with the consequences of how that time is used rather than how much time is actually spent. That is, as a customer, you're buying *results*—or outputs—rather than time, or inputs. It's not that price doesn't matter; it's that results matter more.

These professional outputs have two dimensions: tangible and intangible. Financial statements, tax returns, legal briefs, and glossy presentations are tangible forms of output, which offer evidence that the provider actually did the work. As a customer, however, you are

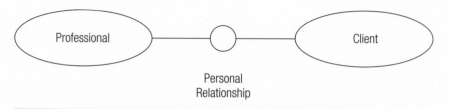

Figure 2-2   **PSF Business Model: A Professional and a Client**

purchasing far more than documents. You want to feel confident and to be reassured that your money is being well managed, that your taxes have been minimized, that your estate plan is solid. You may want someone to brainstorm with or to share personal concerns. Over time, you may solicit advice on a wide array of issues. As mutual respect and trust build, the intangible value of your professional relationship will also grow.

What about the professional who is at the other end of this transaction? He's selling his time, and there are only so many hours in a week. As a service provider, his economics turn on how much time he can bill and at what rate. In his world, time really *is* money! If he has to invest time to sell new clients, his utilization suffers, which is one reason that customer loyalty is so important in professional services. Retained clients are more profitable, both because retention reduces selling costs and because strong client relationships generate the levels of understanding that allow the professional to be more productive (and usually get better results).

Individual professionals live in a world without backlogs. They may have informal agreements or even contracts with their clients, but customers can walk whenever they please. The service provider might complain but, in the end, has little recourse. This reality plus the limited number of hours that any individual has to sell make accomplished professionals acutely sensitive to their customer's needs. If those needs aren't met, their utilization and personal income suffer immediately. For an independent professional, *customer satisfaction* is not an abstract corporate concept, it is what pays the mortgage. Rarely in business is there such a tight and responsive relationship between a service provider and a customer.

Furthermore, the accountability for customer satisfaction is all his, and his alone. He is the marketing department, the sales force, and the manufacturing group. He is responsible for quality control and service. Unlike his corporate counterparts, he can't do any finger pointing at other functions or departments when problems arise. All he can do is yell into the mirror.

Problems (that is, unhappy customers) can cripple his business directly and indirectly. Directly, he loses fees. Indirectly, his identity in the marketplace suffers since most professional work is generated by word of mouth. When potential clients inquire, his past (unhappy) clients will suggest they look elsewhere for services. In all likelihood, he'll never even know that he lost a shot at new business.

This word-of-mouth dynamic works both ways, which is another reason strong relationships with customers are so critical to professional service providers. Professionals need to build customer loyalty; their business depends on it. They are not simply selling time: They are selling *themselves*—a combination of expertise, insight, trust, perhaps even friendship. With satisfied customers, their business and income will grow. As they find themselves fully utilized (or sold out), they will be able to raise prices. As long as they deliver the results clients want, they will prosper.

In strong professional–client relationships, a mutual dependency develops between provider and customer. Each needs the other and helps contribute to the health of the relationship. Trust is a two-way street, as are respect and commitment. What might appear to be a transactional economic exchange (money for time) is, in reality, much more because the relationship is grounded in benefits that extend beyond each party's P&L. The buyer's reward is greater satisfaction and better results, while the seller enhances his capabilities and reputation. The enduring customer loyalty that can ensue epitomizes the kind of customer relationship to which many corporations aspire.

The PSF Business Model: From One Professional to Many

The PSF business model becomes much more complex when you move from a single provider and his client to a firm composed of dozens (or hundreds) of partners, supported by hundreds (or thousands) of more junior professionals and staff. Issues of scale aside, the primary reason for the complexity is that this change introduces a second critical variable into the business model: the behavior of the individual professional toward his colleagues and firm (see figure 2-3).

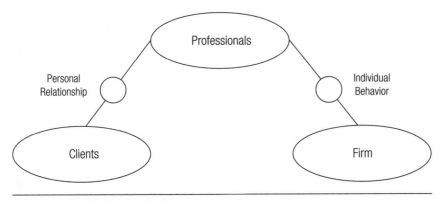

Figure 2-3   **PSF Business Model:**
Professionals—Their Clients and Their Firms

As members of a firm, accomplished professionals play three distinct roles. They are *producers* who sell business and serve clients. They are *managers*, in that they must help to run the firm. They are *owners* with a long-term interest in the firm. They may share their firm's values and perspectives on the business in a general sense, but on any given issue or any given day, the views of an individual partner may differ dramatically from those of the firm. He may disagree about which clients he should serve, the quality and level of resources the firm provides for him, or how the firm evaluates and rewards his contribution. He may want to invest less cash in certain firm initiatives or dissent from recent partner promotions. He may respect some colleagues and detest others.

The strength of the firm overall lies in its ability to shape the behavior of its individual professionals such that, on average, they put the interests of the firm ahead of their own needs. The larger the proportion of partners who are willing to do this, the more aligned the firm will be—and the higher the odds that it will achieve its objectives over time, even though any single individual may fall short. Conversely, the smaller the proportion of professionals who put the firm first, the greater the likelihood that sooner or later the firm will fail.

When accomplished professionals consistently put their own needs ahead of the firm's, the consequences are quickly apparent. Bickering becomes epidemic. Productivity declines. Individual partners begin leaving for better opportunities. Finally, groups begin to spin off to form competing firms.

This scenario was acted out in the death of Gaston & Snow in 1991. The venerable 170-year-old law firm, Boston's fifth largest, with almost 300 lawyers, ended up in bankruptcy court. The reason? Some partners put their personal financial interests ahead of the firm's interest, and no one was able to exert the leadership to resolve the problem. As one former partner summed it up, "An excellent firm was less than the sum of its parts."[5]

The financial consequences of this chain of events are equally destructive. Revenue declines when accomplished professionals leave because it takes years to grow a high-performing partner who fits with the values and culture of a firm and such people are not easily replaced. In addition, as the senior people leave, they usually try to recruit the younger professionals whom they know do the best work. As more departures occur, morale and productivity decline, further depressing profits. New business erodes as clients follow professionals to other firms. Eventually, reductions in cash flow reduce compensation at the senior level, making the firm vulnerable to still more departures.

To complicate the issue further, the balance of power between the firm and its accomplished professionals tilts sharply toward the latter—another distinct characteristic of the PSF business model. Unlike most corporations, PSFs are highly dependent on the retention and productivity of their senior producers. In a corporate environment, if the vice president of marketing or manufacturing quits, it may be a loss, but a search firm will help fill the vacancy in a few months. Customers will not respond directly to the executive's departure by purchasing less; revenue will be largely unaffected. Younger employees, rather than being devastated, may secretly rejoice as positions open up within the corporate structure.

The general marketability of professionals further skews the balance of power in their favor. These are highly educated and mobile individuals. They can switch firms or decide to hang out their own shingles. The nature of their work builds a strong network of personal contacts, including clients who may be interested in recruiting them.

As any successful firm well knows, you can never take these people for granted.

The PSF Business Model: The Firm and Its Marketplace

The third and final dimension of the PSF business model is the interface between the firm and the marketplace of clients (figure 2-4). Whereas the first two dimensions (the professional's relationship to his clients and his behavior toward his colleagues and firm) are predominantly personal, the third dimension is primarily institutional. It is institutional in that it reflects the firm's strategy relative to the marketplace: which set of customers' needs the firm intends to address, with what set of capabilities, and against which competitors. It is also personal in that this strategy has to be implemented by those same individual professionals who are responsible for building client relationships and behaving as constructive members of the community.

For example, who is accountable for following through when a firm decides to pursue new industries to increase revenues? The professional staff. Who is most affected if a firm decides to merge or shut down an office? The professional staff—who are also major owners. If

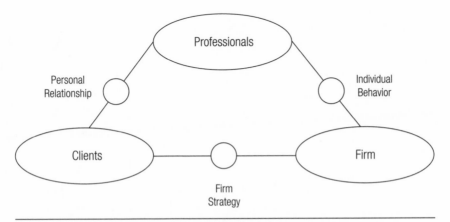

Figure 2-4   **PSF Business Model: Professionals, Clients, and Firm**

a firm wants to change its pricing strategy, who is accountable for the implementation? The professionals who personally price every project they sell. In PSFs, accomplished professionals have enormous control over the implementation of strategy.

In traditional corporations, the corporate center or business unit managers design the strategy, which is subsequently implemented in the field across various functions and locations. While there is usually some participation and, one hopes, consensus building, the decisions are typically top-down, where "top" refers to a handful of senior executives.

In the case of PSFs, the field and the corporate center are essentially one and the same, since each partner-level professional is an owner who simultaneously sells and services clients while helping to lead the firm. Consensus and buy-in are therefore imperative in getting individuals to follow through on strategic decisions. The "top" of the firm comprises dozens, hundreds, maybe even thousands of people. Once again, the firm must shape the behavior of relatively independent professionals, motivating them to achieve its goals.

The central difference—and distinguishing characteristic—of the PSF business model is its reliance, its absolute dependence, on skilled and motivated professionals. Firms that attract and retain the best people and motivate them to build enduring client relationships, put the firm first, and follow through on strategic imperatives are the firms that ultimately win.

Not Just People, But Stars

"People are our most important asset" is a hackneyed phrase in business. A more accurate and honest statement in many industries might be "competent people are a necessary component of our success." Why? Because important as a company's people are, they are usually somewhat expendable. The reason is simple. In most businesses a company's competitive advantage does not rely *directly* on the retention, motivation, and behavior of particular individuals. Instead, it turns on shelf space, brand strength, cost position, distribution systems, price, technology, product design, location, or any number of other variables that can exist apart from the individuals who created them. So except in the long term, most companies' profit performance does not necessarily correlate with their "people assets."

Not so for professional service firms. These firms depend not just on "people assets," but on *stars*. Who are an organization's stars? They are the individuals who have the highest future value to the organization, the men and women in critical jobs whose performance is central to the company's success. If a star leaves, the firm and its clients notice the difference. If enough stars leave, the firm's financial performance suffers. In a law firm, the partners responsible for significant clients, practice areas, and offices are among the stars. At a technology firm, stars may be engineers as well as senior executives. In an advertising agency, world-class "creatives" fit the bill.

In PSFs, stars are typically "partners," but not all partners are stars, nor are all stars partners. (Throughout this book, when we use the term *partner*, we are referring to all the senior executives in a PSF whatever their titles.) What makes PSF stars "stars" is the fact that they propel the business model along all three of its dimensions: building enduring client relationships, consistently performing up to their full potential and putting the firm first, and implementing strategic imperatives. Because they are so accomplished, other members of the firm emulate their behavior.

How many stars does a PSF need? It depends on the industry, the structure of client assignments (for example, the ratio of senior to junior people on a project), and the competition. Stars must be defined by calibrating against the primary competitors' talent as well as against peers in their own firm. Why? Being a B student in a class of C students does not make one a star—although it may appear so for a while. At the end of the day, client perspectives matter most. In the marketplace for professional services, clients decide which individuals are great versus which are just good. In boom times, when services are in high demand, some clients may have to settle for mediocre providers because of capacity constraints (the industry's stars are fully utilized elsewhere). But when the economy turns down, and demand for services dips, stars are freed up to compete; as a consequence, star-rich firms gain share.

Whatever the number of stars, however, in the firms that lead their industries and perform admirably year after year, two things are true. The vast majority of seasoned professionals are stars, and a significant (but smaller) percentage of junior professionals are also stars relative to their peer group. The former happy situation is a direct consequence of the latter: the success of a PSF hinges on the growth and development of a constant stream of star talent. This is why professionals who excel at selling business while simultaneously destroying subordinates are never truly stars. Some supersalesmen, or "rainmakers," may look like stars, but only if the firm focuses solely on the revenues they generate without accounting for the costs they inflict—in poor morale, lower productivity, turnover among junior stars, and, worst of all, the insidious undermining of core firm values.

Are stars perfect? Of course not. Every human being has strengths and weaknesses, and stars are no exception. The question is whether these weaknesses are addressed systematically, throughout a professional's career, so that they don't get out of hand and undermine their potential. Rainmakers, for example, often get more satisfaction from building client relationships than they do from developing younger associates. What distinguishes the rainmakers who are stars from those who aren't is that the former not only strengthen their firm's top line but also are sufficiently aligned with its goals and values to manage the way they behave with colleagues. To state it simply, they put the firm first.

As this suggests, employing stars is necessary but insufficient. They must also be aligned; that is, they must behave in ways that move the firm toward its goals, even if this is at their own expense. Unfortunately, such behavior is usually an unnatural act. This is particularly true in PSFs, where the professionals' natural independence is compounded by the inherently decentralized nature of the work. Accomplished professionals want to run their own business alongside their colleagues. They want to sell and serve their own clients, choose the work they do, and decide how to do it. Most entered professional services—and prospered—because of a desire and ability to "do their own thing" professionally while affiliating with like-minded people.

Yet in a firm (or any organization, for that matter) where everyone "does their own thing," there will be more than a little chaos—there will be underperformance. When a firm whose stars are aligned encounters an unaligned firm in the marketplace, the aligned firm will win the majority of contests. Why? Because the aligned firm is competing on the basis of its entire organization—its "team"—while the unaligned firm fields only individually motivated stars. In today's highly competitive market for professional services, alignment has become more important than ever before.

Turmoil Today, Problems—and Opportunities—Tomorrow

The environment in which PSFs do business has changed fundamentally in the past two decades, and it is still changing—perhaps faster than people realize. The market forces propelling these changes will affect every type of professional service, creating massive opportunities and unforeseen crises. And there is no going back—as the marketplace evolves so must the firms that compete in it.

Overall market growth is dramatically expanding the potential for PSFs, as we noted earlier. In addition, traditional business boundaries are blurring. Professional service firms, once so neatly defined by specialty, are surging into new businesses. PricewaterhouseCoopers bought up European law firms and emerged as one of the world's largest legal service providers. (Its legal practice, Landwell, employs 1,500 business lawyers in 40 countries.) Korn/Ferry launched Futurestep, an Internet search business in partnership with *The Wall Street Journal*. McKinsey opened business technology offices to challenge IT consulting firms, while IBM Global Services offered the "Dot-Com Dozen" package to Web start-ups. American Management Systems, the massive IT consulting firm, teamed up with Barclay's Bank and others to form a new venture aimed at improving banks' processing of financial transactions. WPP acquired an array of advertising and marketing firms and pitches "strategic marketing services" to chief executives. Brash youngsters such as Sapient and Diamond Cluster challenged older premier firms in strategic consulting. Systems integrator EDS aggressively entered consulting through its $300 million acquisition of A.T. Kearney. Meanwhile, technology giant Cisco snapped up 20 percent of KPMG Consulting.[6]

Growth industries typically attract new competitors, and professional services are no exception. The world is awash in PSFs. Despite some consolidation, especially among the largest firms, 2,600 (net) new accounting firms entered the competitive landscape during the 1990s, such that by the end of 2000 there were 11,000 U.S. firms. Executive search firms leapt from 3,560 to 5,490 competitors. In 1990 there were relatively few technology-related PSFs. Today there are 16,200 public and private firms providing technical services in the U.S. alone. In the past decade, over 2,300 new advertising firms entered the marketplace. Freelance consultants in the U.S. increased in number from 1,400 in 1990 to an astonishing 50,000 in 2000.[7]

Growth industries also attract capital. The boom in mergers and acquisitions (M&A) activity is telling. This trend indicates just how aggressively professional firms are investing to strengthen their competitive positions and penetrate new market segments and geographies. Price Waterhouse merged with Coopers & Lybrand. Alex Brown, America's oldest investment bank, was acquired by Bankers Trust—which in turn was acquired by Deutsche Bank. The consulting arm of Ernst & Young was sold to Cap Gemini. An American law firm, Rogers and Wells, grabbed both the British firm Clifford Chance and a German firm, Puender, Volhard. Korn/Ferry completed ten acquisitions in fewer than two years. Interpublic agreed to purchase True North for $2 billion. Publicis S.A. (the French communication, public relations, and advertising group) acquired Saatchi & Saatchi. WPP acquired Young & Rubicam (one of seventy-three acquisitions in 1999–2000).

The big deals make headlines while smaller transactions go unnoticed, yet the totals are staggering. Between 1985 and 1990 there were 1,140 professional service firm M&A deals in the United States alone. Between 1995 and 2000 that number climbed to a record 7,638. The total transaction value for those two periods rocketed from $27 billion to $471 billion—a seventeenfold increase (see figure 2-5)![8] Few sectors

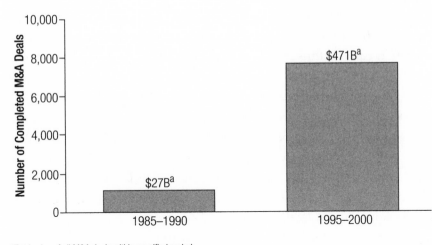

aTotal value of all M&A deals within specified period.
Source: SDC database; *Consultants News*.

Figure 2-5 **Professional Service Firms' M&A Activity,
1985–1990, 1995–2000**

of the American economy have experienced such a surge in transaction activity.

Capital is invested not only to acquire firms but also to recruit individuals. Starting salaries in large U.S. law firms jumped 30 percent in a single year (1999–2000). Private consulting firms such as Bain & Company offer investment equity to better attract and retain star consultants. Publicly traded firms pile stock options on top of cash bonuses. Over 60 percent of Harvard Business School graduates entered the professional service sector in 2000; the average median compensation package for these graduates approached $150,000.[9]

The best people, it turns out, are expensive. For professional firms, the "war for talent" is actually a war for stars. This war never stops among the leading professional firms and is particularly fierce today because so many other businesses (technology companies, for example) are competing for the same skills and brains.

Historically, PSF growth was funded exclusively by partner capital, augmented by occasional lines of credit. The roaring stock markets of the 1990s prompted new sources of financing. Dot-com consultants jumped on the IPO bandwagon and created an industry segment that exploded from nowhere to an aggregate market capitalization of $63 billion in early 2000—before plummeting below $4 billion by the fall of 2001. Old-line firms, in an effort to bolster their competitive position (and professional rewards), launched their own IPOs. KPMG spun off its consulting business in a 2001 public offering. Young & Rubicam sold shares to Hellman & Friedman (a private equity firm), went public in 1988, and sold to WPP in 2000. Watson Wyatt Worldwide, a leading human resource consulting firm, launched an IPO that same year. Total IPO activity by PSFs increased more than fivefold during the back half of the 1990s (see figure 2-6).[10]

As firms invest to pursue growth opportunities, scale and complexity multiply. In 1975, McKinsey & Company had 24 office locations; today it has 81. Korn/Ferry had 25 offices in 1970; it has over 75 today. By 2000, Grey Worldwide had a presence in 97 countries. IBM Global Services now encompasses over 150,000 employees serving in 150 countries—almost half of IBM's total employees. PricewaterhouseCoopers boasts a partnership of over 10,000 individuals.

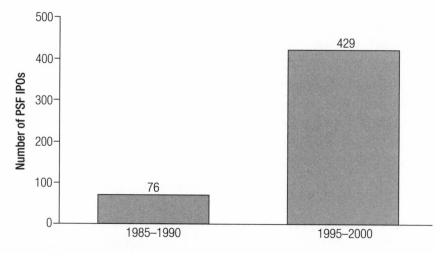

Source: SDC New Issues Database.

Figure 2-6   **Professional Service Firm's IPO Activity, 1985–1990, 1995–2000**

Skadden Arps became the first law firm ever to top $1 billion in annual revenue during 1999.

As clients globalize, many PSFs follow or select a specific segment within which to compete. In 1998, Linklaters brought together five of Europe's top law firms to form Linklaters & Alliance, a consortium of over 3,000 lawyers in 34 offices worldwide. In contrast, Brobeck, Phleger & Harrison is focused on serving U.S. technology companies. In 1999 it ranked twenty-second on *American Lawyer*'s list of top 100 law firms, generating $855,000 in profits per partner.[11] As firms expand geographic strategies, target clients, and value propositions, competition naturally intensifies. As the saying goes, "Every day you are either gaining or losing share—whether you know it or not." Consequently, professional firms are exhibiting some unusual behavior such as advertising their services. Accenture spent $175 million rebranding itself after it split from Andersen. Ernst & Young spent almost $100 million on advertising in 2000; KPMG spent $60 million. Even old-line law firms like Boston's Hale and Dorr are running ads. Web sites proliferate, promising clients cures for whatever ails them, from "delivering quantifiable results" (Accenture) to "offering a full spectrum of services in strategy, systems, operations, and technology" (Booz•Allen & Hamilton).

Information technology further amplifies this competitive dynamic. Technology creates new consulting markets like e-business services. Technology encourages the obsolescence of professional services that can be easily commoditized (the software program Turbo Tax, for example). Technology reduces service cycle times; gone are the days of lengthy projects with distant checkpoints. Whether it is e-mail, extranets, or knowledge management, technology is transforming professional services. Online recruitment, for example, has tripled in the past three years, and it was expected to exceed $2 billion in 2001. Even online self-service consulting is expanding. Ernst & Young launched "Earnie" in 1996 to provide cost-effective business solutions to clients online. The Internet routes client questions to the consultants at Ernst & Young best suited to address specific inquiries. Subscribers can also search databases of prior answers or access consulting tools such as a supply chain diagnostic. The most striking example of a new technical age may be illustrated by the staid and quiet world of private banking. Goldman Sachs launched GS.com to serve its high–net worth clients, while J.P. Morgan reciprocated with Morgan Online.[12]

Market growth, competition, consolidation, new entrants, diversification, globalization, technology—business turmoil abounds. For PSFs accustomed to being "above the fray," this is an astonishing experience. Studies of industries in turmoil are quite conclusive: Businesses rarely maintain the status quo. Either they capture the opportunities or they are pummeled by the risks.[13] In such an environment, even the best and longest-lived firm cannot move forward without an explicit competitive strategy. The next chapter discusses why this is so and what you and your firm can do to develop such a strategy.

3 ★ Strategy

Necessary but Not Sufficient

JACK KNEW *he was in trouble. As chair of the strategy task force, he was slated to present the white paper outlining the firm's proposed new strategy at next week's annual partner meeting. He hadn't wanted the assignment in the first place, but the managing partner had persuaded him that it would be a unique high-profile opportunity and an outstanding learning experience. In fact, he had learned a lot over the past six months. He'd learned that his task force members preferred client work to strategic thinking. He'd learned that his partners disagreed about almost everything strategic—including the very definition of strategy as it applied to their firm. He'd learned that personal agendas, local interests, and generational differences made objective discussion of strategic issues almost impossible.*

Some partners believed fervently in the strength of the firm—that their downturn was just another business cycle and that all they really needed to do was hunker down and stick to the basics, which had served them so well over the years. In sharp contrast, other partners believed the firm was breaking (if not already broken)—that their marketplace was changing rapidly and that if they didn't change with it they'd perish. This latter contingent didn't agree among themselves on the central problem or what to do. Should they diversify into new services? Expand into new locations? Target different customers? Which, if any, competitors posed the greatest threat? Perhaps it was time to merge with a competitor, or at least forge a strategic alliance.

Underlying every discussion were the issues of money and ownership: How would a new strategy affect partner compensation? How would major initiatives be funded? Should they sell all or part of the firm? Should they go public?

It was inconceivable that his white paper could build consensus around these complex questions. Everyone was smart and had a strong opinion (especially the senior partners). Unfortunately, there were few objective facts available to alter all these closely held beliefs.

Meanwhile, the marketplace wasn't waiting for them to choose a new course of action. Competitors were merging, selling out, entering new lines of business, and opening new offices overseas. New competitors, new technologies, and new approaches seemed to appear monthly. Perhaps all this change was a short-term blip, but it certainly didn't feel that way.

Even if his partners could decide on a strategy, he had little confidence that they would follow through on their decisions. The firm was so decentralized, and the partners so client-focused that most likely little would actually change. People would go back to work selling and serving their traditional clients, while they grumbled about the shortcomings of the firm and its leadership.

The more he reflected, the more depressed he became. The white paper was a waste of time, and the exposure it gave him might do his career more harm than good. He couldn't wait to return to full-time client work himself!

Strategy in Professional Service Firms

Strategy is about achieving a firm's goals and winning in the marketplace. Every business has some sort of strategy, although in professional service firms (PSFs) it is as likely to be implicit as explicit. When times are good, there is a natural tendency to believe that your firm's strategy—however incomplete or ill conceived it may be—is working well. In difficult times (often marked by revenue shortfalls), the opposite is true: Strategy emerges as the culprit. Debate intensifies within the firm, followed by strategic task forces, strategic studies, and strategic proclamations. These activities may or may not produce decisions that improve the firm's performance; often, especially in PSFs, they fail to achieve any result other than time-consuming distraction.

Strategy is not an episodic phenomenon—it is *always* critical to an enterprise's long-term success. The best firms understand this, thinking and acting strategically in good times as well as bad. Doing so requires a clear definition of strategy and an understanding of its central elements.

If you've spent any time in the business section of a bookstore, you know that strategy has tens, if not hundreds, of competing definitions. These range from the precepts of military strategists like Sun Tzu (*The Art of War*, written between the fifth and eighth centuries B.C., is a perennial business bestseller) to the frameworks of contemporary economists like Michael Porter. The definition we think is most helpful—especially for PSFs—comes from Ken Andrews, one of the founding fathers of the field.

Andrews defined *strategy* as a stream of decisions made over time, which reflects the goals of the firm and the means by which the firm achieves those goals.[1] This definition underscores the inherently dynamic nature of strategy. It reminds us that strategy goes beyond planning exercises and formal five-year plans, that it plays out daily as an organization and its environment evolve. Strategy doesn't live in isolation, up on a mountaintop, shrouded in clouds, tended by almighty thinkers. It lives all over the mountain, as professionals throughout the firm pursue goals and make decisions each day. Strategy is as much about *doing* as it is about thinking. So Andrews's definition is useful because it keeps us pointed in the right direction, focused on substance rather than form, on reality rather than a plan.

Goals

The "stream of decisions made over time" begins with the firm's goals. Goals reflect the ambitions of the enterprise and its owners, the hoped-for point of arrival along whatever dimensions are most important to the firm and its owners. Goals run the gamut from aspirations such as "being the best in the world at what we do" to "helping our clients outperform their competitors." They may also include aspects of financial performance or firm character, for instance, to increase profit per partner while retaining the attributes of a small local firm. Whatever the specifics, a firm's goals should reinforce its values and highlight the few unique circumstances that will affect its future most deeply.

The firm's goals set the stage for a series of interrelated choices that its leadership must make. These *strategic choices* define how the firm will differentiate itself from its competitors, who its target clients will be, and the nature of the value proposition the firm will offer to them. The relationships among these elements are depicted in the strategy pyramid in figure 3-1. We'll look at each of them in turn.

Competitive Differentiation

In a competitive marketplace, winning requires that a business serve some set of customer needs better than its competitors. In the competitive market for professional services, the same principle applies: Clients award their business to one firm rather than another because they think that the winning firm will do a better job. In the vocabulary of strategy, the winning firm is *differentiated* along one or more dimensions that matter significantly in its clients' eyes. This differentiation

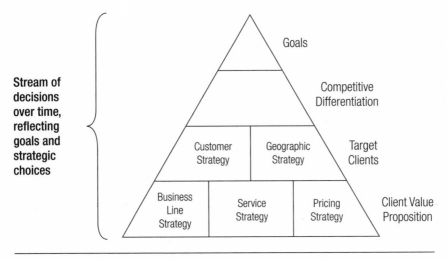

Stream of decisions over time, reflecting goals and strategic choices

Goals

Competitive Differentiation

Customer Strategy

Geographic Strategy

Target Clients

Business Line Strategy

Service Strategy

Pricing Strategy

Client Value Proposition

Figure 3-1 **Strategy Pyramid**

can be explicit and concrete (for example, "they are a well-established local firm with two offices in my city"). Or it can be subtle and intangible (for example, "I like their style"). In either case, differentiation is what gives the firm its competitive advantage.

The level of competitive differentiation among professional service providers varies noticeably depending on their industry's dynamics, including its degree of consolidation. Historically, PSFs were more often differentiated by intangible factors than by direct comparisons with competitors. This still tends to be the case in industries such as legal services that are highly fragmented (see figure 3-2). In more consolidated industries such as accounting, however, it is possible to achieve competitive advantage against specifically named competitors. For example, Price Waterhouse merged with Coopers & Lybrand so that it could compete more effectively on a global basis with its arch rival, Andersen Worldwide. It implemented a competitive strategy in part designed to outflank Andersen in Europe.

In less consolidated industries, competitive differentiation occurs within clusters of competitors. Hundreds of firms provide strategy consulting services, for instance. However, the three so-called top-tier global firms, McKinsey, Bain, and the Boston Consulting Group, frequently find themselves competing directly for the same client

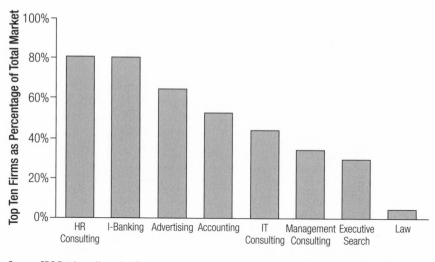

Source: SDC Database; Kennedy Information; Consulting Central Web site; AdAge Web site; Gross Billings; Accountancy International Network report (1999 and 2000); Public Accounting National Firms report (1995); *Consultants News; Executive Recruiter News; American Lawyer.*

Figure 3-2   Industry Consolidation 2000

business. Clients foster this competition by soliciting proposals from all three firms for similar types of work. In these situations, clients define the industry's competitive boundaries, and the firms must respond accordingly, with the differentiation among them becoming critical to their success.

Target Clients

In professional services, the adage that no two customers are exactly alike is especially apt. Recall the first dimension of the PSF business model: the individual client served by the individual professional. A client (the head of marketing who buys services from an advertising agency, for example) represents his organization, but he is also representing himself—his own needs and perspectives. As a result, the firm's competitive differentiation depends on its ability to fully meet the specific business *and* individual needs of certain customers.

The question "Who are our target clients?" is therefore both critical and complex for a firm. It requires explicit decisions about client priorities. For example, which industries are most important to serve? What type of clients within these industries: Large or small? Stagnant or growing? Bureaucratic or entrepreneurial? Furthermore, which *individuals* in those client businesses are the buyers with whom the firm can realistically hope to forge a relationship? Are they junior or senior? Line or staff? At the corporate center or in the field? Conservative or risk takers? How many of them will be involved in the decision?

These client-related questions lead directly to issues of geographic strategy. To what extent can or should a firm remain local? Or national? What level of presence is required to compete effectively in large markets like the United States or Germany? What exactly does being "global" mean—a presence in five countries or twenty-five? Can that presence be achieved through joint ventures and alliances, or must a firm grow painstakingly from within?

The strategic decisions surrounding a firm's target clients are therefore bound up in issues of geographc strategy as well as customer differentiation. These elements lead directly to the final element of strategy: the value proposition a firm offers its targeted clients in its chosen geographies.

Client Value Proposition

The concept of a *value proposition* is deceptively simple because at one level it equates with the lines of business in which a firm engages (accounting services, for example, or Web design). Yet the client is purchasing a *service*, which implies a certain level of attention as well as a particular kind of capability. Do you meet with the client every day or monthly? Your office or theirs? Do you involve three client executives in the service process or thirty? Do you staff your project with a heavy mix of experienced professionals, or do you deploy a single senior partner supported by specialists and young analysts?

The true value proposition to your client is all-inclusive, encompassing both the comprehensive service you provide (an audit, an ad campaign, an information system) and the process with which you provide it. In addition, because it is the entire experience of working with an outside professional that matters to the client, your firm's value proposition has a personal element as well. This personal value element is critical to the person purchasing the professional service. Will this effort make her look good to senior management or the board of directors? Will it help advance her career? Will she learn from the experience? Will it be fun?

One thing is certain: The experience doesn't come free. How professionals price their services is a critical strategic issue for two reasons: It helps define the client value proposition (value at a price), and it drives the firm's economics (along with utilization). Pricing strategy involves many related issues: Do you quote a fee for the project or price your services on an hourly basis? If it's on a project fee basis, how are overruns and changes of scope accommodated? Is your fee to be paid entirely in cash, or is there a non-cash component such as equity? Is there a performance incentive built into your contract? Do you price differently by geography, by business line, or by customer segment? Do you price differently against different competitors?

From a client's perspective, moreover, these economic aspects of pricing don't tell the entire story. Clients encounter another type of "price" as well: the time, effort, and risk associated with engaging an outside service provider at all. For the client company, an assignment could require allocating people to the project, creating special task forces, or participating in meetings and retreats. For the individual executive, too, the price extends well beyond the cash his company pays the firm contrasted with the services it receives in return. It could mean significant incremental duties layered on an already hectic schedule. It could mean disrupted relationships with coworkers, or potential embarrassment if things don't go well. At worst, it could damage a promising career.

Developing an integrated strategy (comprising the firm's goals, competitive differentiation, target clients, and client value proposition) requires explicit *choices* among the various possibilities confronting a firm over time. Choices involve tradeoffs: doing one thing (pursuing clients in an unfamiliar industry, for instance) and not doing something else (not opening new European offices). Because every firm's resources are finite, strategic decisions always involve what *not* to do as well as what is to be done. In fact, two of the best indicators of a functioning strategy are how often and under what circumstances a firm and its leadership say "No" to attractive (but nonstrategic) opportunities.

Using strategy to choose among activities is critical in PSFs where so many individuals have the freedom to say "Yes" to what appear to be personally interesting and profitable opportunities—even if those opportunities are inconsistent with the firm's goals.

Stars and Strategy

Just as business enterprises have goals, so too do the individuals they employ. In the case of PSFs, the two are entwined because the professionals who manage, lead, and own shares in the firm are the same people who compete in the marketplace for clients.

Stars—the individuals who have the highest future value to the firm—are central to making the firm's strategy real by implementing its strategic decisions and pursuing its strategic goals. At the same time, they are more or less independently minded sole practitioners, who can have an alarming tendency to do whatever they want regardless of the wishes of the firm's leaders. Stars don't follow directions particularly well. Immersed in client work, they may not pay attention to strategic pronouncements. Even if they do, they may not care enough to modify their behavior; apathy can be an enormous barrier to implementing firm strategy. Finally, they may decide not to follow the new imperatives simply because they *don't want to* given their own circumstances and goals.

In essence, accomplished professionals have their own strategy pyramids, which rarely overlap perfectly with their firms' strategic goals. The elements are similar, but the content is strikingly different. For each individual, the pyramid includes:

Goals: My professional and personal ambitions.

Competitive differentiation: My strengths and how I can build on them; my weaknesses and how I can compensate for them or shore them up.

Target clients: What clients I personally want to serve and with whom I have a relationship. Where I want to live and work.

Client value proposition: What capabilities I provide my clients, with what level of service, at what fees.

The tension between institutional strategy (a firm's goals and decisions) and individual strategy (a professional's goals and decisions) is an inherent characteristic of the PSF business model described in chapter 2. The problem is that ultimately, it is the behavior of stars in the context of their client and firm relationships that determines the efficacy of the firm's strategy (see figure 3-3).

When conflicts between individual stars and the firm intensify, strategic decisions are likely to be incompletely implemented, delayed, or ignored. The efforts of one, midsized multinational firm to implement a new geographic strategy offer a case in point.

After years of study and debate, the firm had finalized its geographic strategy. The senior partners who led the effort had achieved consensus on the new direction: The firm would take a portfolio approach to globalization, with a different priority assigned to each nation based on its market size and the firm's own competitive position. In aggregate, there were more opportunities than resources, so the partners carefully drew hard-and-fast boundaries around geographies the firm would *not* enter, virtually all of which were emerging markets.

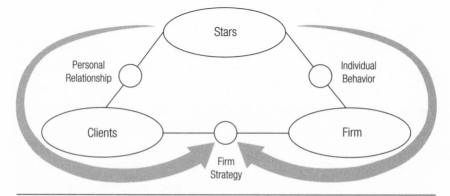

Figure 3-3 **Stars Drive Strategy**

Overall, the geographic strategy made sense to almost everyone in the firm. Even partners working in some of the lower-priority national markets accepted the premise that the firm should invest disproportionately in high-potential countries.

The PowerPoint presentation had barely faded, however, before the strategy began to unravel. The unraveling had nothing to do with lack of understanding or misguided intentions. It simply occurred as relatively autonomous partners pursued individual opportunities that made sense to them.

Partners in Frankfurt landed a huge privatization project in the Czech Republic. While the Czech Republic was not a geographic priority (and, in fact, was "out of bounds"), the office head could not say "no" to her senior colleague, especially when the office needed the business. Within eighteen months, the Czech revenue had tripled and a number of partners were camped out in Prague full-time. Revenue generated in Germany (a high-priority market) languished, as more and more of the office was drawn into Czech client assignments.

On the other side of the globe, the senior partner leading the firm's worldwide technology practice was invited to address a conference of Indian CEOs. After an outstanding speech, he was invited to return to India—a country he'd always enjoyed. During the subsequent trip, a number of the CEOs badgered him about his firm's lack of presence in such an enormous marketplace. (India, too, was deemed strategically out of bounds.) By now, the intrepid partner had become sold on India (and saw an outstanding career opportunity for himself). After selling projects to three companies, he returned triumphantly to the London office full of enthusiasm and commitment.

Meanwhile, the successful head of the Los Angeles office had decided to return to his native Brazil. He wanted to remain an active member of the partnership, but had to move for personal reasons. Although Brazil was also out of bounds because of the firm's limited resources, it had done business in South America on rare occasions for multinational clients. So after multiple conversations, the managing partner not only agreed to keep his old friend on the payroll but also approved the lease of a tiny office in São Paulo. With the office came a secretary and, later, a few junior professionals who transferred for six to twelve months on temporary assignment. Once again, the firm—in the person of its CEO—had violated its carefully considered geographic strategy.

Is this opportunistic behavior inappropriate? *Yes,* in that it diverts scarce resources away from strategic priorities and adds unnecessary complexity to an already complex business. *No,* in that retaining and motivating stars are a firm's primary imperatives, and that means coping with their independent tendencies. This is part of the never-ending balancing act between the firm's goals and its professionals' goals. In an environment in which people would rather ask forgiveness than permission, designing and implementing an effective strategy can be both frustrating and risky.

Consider what happened when NationsBank, the third largest bank in the United States, acquired Thomas Weisel's Montgomery Securities, an entrepreneurial West Coast investment bank focused on high-growth industries such as technology and telecommunications. In October 1997, NationsBank spent $1.2 billion to acquire Montgomery and form NationsBank Montgomery, which it hoped would become a lucrative investment bank within the parent corporation. The conflicts began almost immediately. Weisel and his colleagues thought they had an agreement with their new parent to manage specific activities (including high-yield bonds, equity investing, and services such as LBO funds to big investors) from San Francisco. NationsBank executives wanted to manage those activities mostly from the headquarters in Charlotte as part of the overall banking business.

Loathe to become part of the button-down commercial banking culture and more interested in implementing his own vision of investment banking, Weisel resigned as CEO of NationsBank Montgomery less than a year after the deal closed. In January 1999, he started Thomas Weisel Partners LLC, a boutique merchant bank focused exclusively on emerging growth companies. Weisel wooed former Montgomery employees to join him, and within a week of the firm's founding, he had succeeded in hiring twenty-five people away from NationsBank Montgomery, including the former head of technology investment banking, the former head of business services banking, and a technology mergers and acquisitions specialist. Drawn into battle, NationsBank Montgomery executives rescinded bonuses from junior bankers who waited until the day after the distribution to leave the firm. (Faced with negative reactions, internally and externally, Nations-Bank later restored the bonuses.)

What did NationsBank really get when they bought Montgomery? After so many talented professionals (including the firm's leader) jumped ship, it certainly wasn't the strategic capability they thought they had acquired. The stars were the strategy—a fact that dramatically increased the risk of failure.

Strategic Complexity

The personalities, emotions, and needs of a firm's stars constrain its ability to design and implement strategy. As if that were not enough, other factors further complicate the process.

First, most PSFs compete in many different locations, each of which may require a distinctive mix of strategic decisions. What's right for the United Kingdom may not be right for France, much less Japan. Different competitive environments may even dictate a different strategy for the New York office than the one in St. Louis. Practice areas may also pursue separate combinations of target clients and value propositions; for example, the financial services practice strategy does not need to resemble the strategy for health care.

The number and mix of a firm's businesses are likewise dependent on the competitive dynamics and boundaries of the various markets in which they compete. This means that the definition of those businesses is determined by conditions *outside* the firm, not by internal characteristics such as the firm's organizational structure or financial reporting systems. Most PSFs are diversified across a portfolio of somewhat separate businesses (practices and geographies). The natural desire to create a "one-firm" culture should not mask this harsh strategic reality. A firm's overall strategy must be integrated enough to hang together, while embracing a portfolio of different businesses each with overlapping but distinct strategies.

The complexity of PSF strategy is especially challenging because certain well-accepted concepts about strategy, which are important in other contexts, have limited applicability in this sector. For example, barriers to entry are so low in many professional areas that they're practically nonexistent. Start-ups need skillful, determined professionals more than they need large amounts of capital. There is little to stop restless and talented partners from leaving a firm (along with one or more valuable colleagues—and clients) to hang out their own shingles, just as Weisel did. True, new entrants can struggle, and many disappear or never become more than one-man bands. But while they're around, they heighten the competitive pressure.

Benefits of scale is another loaded concept. In many parts of the professional service sector, firms are growing and consolidating, in part based on a belief in the benefits of scale. Yet there's little hard evidence that bigger *is* better, economically or competitively, in PSFs. Why? Because clients don't value scale unless it directly affects their value proposition. A client doesn't necessarily care whether a firm's local office has fifty or five hundred professionals, for example, but that client does care about the quality of the professionals assigned to their account. Conversely, a multinational client may demand global capability (which implies some scale) but, depending on the type of service, may not care much about the location and number of a firm's offices. For clients, bigger isn't better; better is better!

This point is highlighted each year in various rankings of consulting firms. Consider some of the data for 2000 from *Consultant's News*. Although the figures are only estimates, and the firms profiled compete in a diverse mix of businesses, the numbers do tell a story.[2] For example, the Monitor Company is considered a boutique consulting firm, generating about $300 million of revenue per year with 1,000 consultants. Monitor's performance of $300,000 in revenue per consultant is slightly above that of the well-established Mercer Consulting Group—even though Mercer has 8,200 consultants! Towers Perrin and Hewitt Associates are competing human resource consulting firms, recently ranked number 12 and number 14 in revenue respectively: Towers generating $1.5 billion, and Hewitt $1.3 billion. Towers Perrin employs 7,200 consultants to produce its annual revenue; Hewitt employs 12,000. A third interesting comparison is between Booz•Allen & Hamilton and McKinsey & Company. Both are well-established consulting firms, with highly diverse multinational practices. Booz is bigger, employing 8,500 consultants globally to McKinsey's 7,200. Yet McKinsey's revenue per consultant is $460,000, two and a half times Booz's return of $180,000 per consultant. Time and again, financial comparisons demonstrate the reality that a firm's scale does not correlate with its financial success.

Scale can be problematic—and fail to yield incremental profits—for various reasons. As the firm grows and a sense of intimacy is lost, its stars can become demotivated and leave. Mergers and acquisitions are not only difficult to implement but also extremely costly, in terms of partners' time as well as money. The increased cost and complexity of scale may outweigh any incremental benefits for which clients will be willing to pay. Finally, the need to tailor services to meet unique sets of client needs can wring the potential for incremental profits out of even very large assignments. As Steven Felscher, executive vice president of finance at Grey Advertising, told us: "Creating economies of scale depends on the nature of the client. One of the most famous campaigns in the world has been the Pedigree-breeders campaign for Pedigree dog food. It is Mars, Inc.'s largest single brand, and for years there was one campaign which was based on breeders talking about how good this product is for their dogs. Yet, in order to have it sell, we had to create thirty-five or forty versions of the campaign every six months or so, because each country needed a local breeder, the right kind of dog, and a sense of the mores of the country."

It is also true that in sharp contrast to businesses in which relative market share correlates with profitability, increased share doesn't necessarily yield positive consequences for PSFs. Wachtell, Lipton, Rosen & Katz, for example, is often described as New York's most successful and selective law firm. Small but premium, Wachtell, Lipton, which had 147 lawyers and 66 equity partners in 1999, is consistently one of the nation's most profitable law firms per partner. It has only one office in New York and a reputation for expertise in takeover defenses and other critical corporate matters. Although ranked twenty-seventh in the *American Lawyer* 100 in terms of gross revenue ($298 million) in 1999, Wachtell, Lipton was ranked first in profitability, raking in $3.385 million in profits per partner and $2.025 million in revenue per lawyer. Baker & McKenzie, with 2,477 lawyers and 558 equity partners and gross revenue of $818 million, almost three times that of Wachtell, Lipton, ranked seventy-second in terms of profits per partner. Although Baker & McKenzie has sixty-two offices worldwide and practices that cover the full spectrum of commercial law, it brought in only $485,000 per partner and $330,000 in revenue per lawyer.

In fact, the very concept of relative market share is problematic for PSFs because it rests on precise business boundaries that practically speaking are difficult to define. The question, "What is our market share?" begs another question, "Relative to which competitor, and in what business?" That, in turn, opens up a host of issues around how the firm's business is defined: by geographic boundaries, professional activity, service levels, price, the skills and personality of its people, or even the skills and personality of one person. A portfolio of overlapping businesses, selling mostly intangible professional services, does not easily conform to strategic concepts that originally emanated from manufacturing industries.

Another familiar strategic concept that needs to be taken with a grain of salt is *first-mover advantage:* the notion that innovations can create lasting competitive advantage. Accomplished PSFs develop new offerings all the time. Wachtell, Lipton's Poison Pill, the takeover defense invented by one of its founders, Marty Lipton, is a fine example, as are mortgage-backed securities, which were launched at Salomon Brothers. There's no question these were innovative products. But once publicized and marketed (as they had to be to take off), they were quickly copied by competitors. Similarly, consider how fast a powerful concept like reengineering became "commoditized" and spread beyond the consulting firm, CSC Index, whose principals first developed it. Within months, CSC's well-established competitors were pitching their own versions of reengineering (after attending a three-day CSC conference).

Like it or not, there are few truly proprietary services, patents, or insights that can sustain a professional firm's bottom line. The track toward commoditization isn't as well worn as it is in consumer goods, but it's there. Take "Web enablement," a concept that technology firms such as Oracle developed to make their software useable on the Web. When companies such as Viant and Scient started offering clients Web enablement as a consulting service, they created a niche that distinguished them—briefly—from would-be competitors. Soon hundreds of other firms began to offer the same service. The advantage was gone, almost overnight. Today, Web enablement is only a small part of the service lines offered by firms that are still competitive.

This phenomenon is not confined to cyberspace. Take auditing, for example. There was a time when auditing was a highly specialized, highly valued service. Now it's largely a commodity.

Last but not least, competing on cost is a much less attractive option for PSFs than it is for many other businesses. In PSFs, the lion's share of the cost structure is related to people (followed by space and, increasingly, technology). To attract and retain talented people, you need to offer compensation packages that are at least as good as your competitors'. (In fact, if your costs are too low, it may indicate that you're not investing enough in your stars and are becoming a second-tier player.)

Cost obviously affects profitability—but it does not *drive* profitability. Thoughtfully managing costs, year in and year out, is important. But focusing on having lower costs than your direct competitors will typically not translate into a competitive advantage. *Temporary* emphasis on cost can reflect sound management. In soft economic times, for example, PSF managers may be even more stringent about performance reviews to accelerate turnover and adjust their cost structure. But constant (or thoughtless) "right sizing" reflects a fundamentally weak firm retreating from the marketplace. Professional service firms, like many businesses, cannot "shrink to greatness." Eventually stars will leave the sinking ship, causing quality, firm utilization, and price to fall.

Strategic Risks

Professionals typically like to concentrate on opportunities. The upside of a new strategic initiative—such as moving into a new geography or business line, selling into a new customer segment, acquiring a smaller competitor—can be easy to envision. The risks are far less visible, however. They are also far more important to understand and address.

Strategic risks come in all shapes and sizes, and obviously depend on the particular circumstances of a firm and its marketplace. Generalizations are at best only a starting point for understanding a problem and its consequences. That said, we have observed four types of risk that are common among PSFs. These risks are common because they are unavoidable. They are also incremental and insidious: invisible dangers that often take years to be acknowledged and confronted—by which time it may well be too late.

Strategic Obsolescence

In a rapidly changing environment, yesterday's strategy is seldom the answer to tomorrow's problems. This is obvious, yet time and again firms maintain the status quo (or make half-hearted efforts at strategic change), even in the face of large-scale upheaval in client needs or competitive dynamics. There are at least three understandable reasons for this head-in-the-sand behavior.

First is human nature. People, and professionals are no exception, tend to hang on to the comfort of past practices rather than venture into uncharted territory. In PSFs, a few progressive leaders cannot order the troops forward; instead, the troops themselves (that is, the other stars) must essentially vote with their feet to pursue a new strategic direction. In most corporations, as we said earlier, strategic change can be instigated from the top down. Not so at PSFs, where the top may be a partnership with dozens (or hundreds) of independent practitioners. Absent a crisis, the partners tend to stay on track and support only modest adjustments to the strategy. Innovative or aggressive strategies rarely emerge from people who are satisfied with the status quo.

Money and power are two other factors that exacerbate the risk of strategic obsolescence. Even in tough times, compensation for accomplished stars may exceed their personal needs (not to mention what they could earn elsewhere). Their firm may decay, but their annual income and personal incentives don't motivate them to pursue new strategies. They've already made it; their generation is fine. The next, younger generation of professionals must worry about themselves. Younger generations of stars may be inherently more ambitious and open-minded, yet they typically lack the organizational power to drive strategic change, and so they are forced to go along with the conservatism of their senior colleagues (or leave the firm). Obsolescence sets in because the future generations (with the most to lose) are trumped by their more complacent elders who may be focused on retirement.

The financial impact of strategic obsolescence may not be fully apparent for years. Long-standing client relationships, developed by senior partners, may continue to keep everyone busy. Past reputation may permit the firm to charge a premium price (especially to new clients), even as its service quality declines. The lag between current performance and future momentum can lead firms to react to market changes by doing too little, too late. Yet the symptoms of strategic obsolescence (such as fewer requests for proposals coming in over the transom or more of your top recruiting candidates turning you down) are often plain to see if the firm's leaders are paying attention.

In today's tumultuous professional marketplace, strategic obsolescence can be deadly long before it affects the owners' pocketbooks. In corporate environments, the risk of strategic obsolescence is typically dwarfed by the tendency to pursue greener pastures. Corporations tend to expand aggressively into new businesses, while inadvertently undermining their strategic core, the powerful market position(s) that built their business in the first place.[3] In PSFs, the opposite danger exists because the need for consensus decision making can fatally encumber change. To succeed, every business (PSFs and corporations alike) must balance these opposing tensions to protect their core and stimulate progress.[4]

Strategic Drift

Did you go to amusement parks as a kid? If you did, you may have driven those miniature cars that zoom around twisty outdoor tracks. If it weren't for your "skillful steering," you (and the parent sitting next to you) surely would have perished. Except, that is, for the concrete curbs. Those curbs guided your wheels along the track, so no matter where you steered, you more or less went straight ahead. In fact, the steering wheel often wasn't connected to the tires at all. You could turn left—and go right. Turn right—and drift left. The sense of control was exhilarating, even if it was an illusion.

When it comes to PSFs and their strategies, it can often feel to firm leaders as though the steering wheel isn't connected to the tires either; unfortunately there aren't any concrete curbs to keep a strategy on track. Examples abound. A firm ratifies its new geographic strategy, and within months they've begun to drift from their intended course. Potential new clients are targeted, lengthy account plans are developed, and, a year later, no one has followed up. A committee of partners devises a sophisticated multitiered pricing strategy, customized for various industries and countries, with the intent of improving margins 10 percent. On paper, the approach is brilliant; in reality, partners continue to price their work as they see fit.

Strategic drift occurs because professionals have their own perspectives, independent of what the firm's leaders may think. Professionals view themselves as running their own businesses (after all, it's *their* time and expertise that's being sold to clients). So strategic drift is inherent in the professional service business model. Whether it becomes problematic and costly depends on how it's managed, as the events in a large human resource consulting firm illustrate.

In 1995, a few of the firm's professionals became enamored with the concept of change management. Bored with the firm's traditional benefits programs and compensation studies, they watched competitors offering change management services to clients and saw no reason why their firm couldn't enter this growing and apparently lucrative business.

The professionals cobbled together a selling presentation, which was notably short on past experience, and began pitching clients. Within six months, they were engaged on three small projects, all led by a dynamic senior partner we'll call Lynn. Lynn had decided to focus all her time on change management work, with the dream of building and leading a giant global profit center (and doing well for herself in the process).

A year later, almost fifty professionals were working on a fragmented mix of change management projects—no two of them exactly alike. Their now-elaborate selling presentations were augmented by a series of glossy brochures and a pair of thought pieces designed to demonstrate the firm's powerful change management insights. Given the momentum, Lynn was aggressively soliciting a $25 million investment over three years to build her practice area. By her calculations, change management would be generating more than half of the firm's profits within a decade. Just as important, if the firm failed to pursue this golden opportunity, it would be forever relegated to the mediocre profitability inherent in its older commodity-like services.

Lynn knew about mediocre profitability: The change management practice area was bleeding cash. Tiny projects and long-selling cycles depressed staff utilization, while fees were being slashed to encourage new clients to sign on. The combination was devastating: Including indirect expenses, Lynn's area was losing over $1 million per month. Fortunately for her, the firm's accounting system didn't track net practice area profits accurately, and revenues were continuing to show an upward trend with astonishing growth rates (albeit off a low base).

The firm's executive committee reacted to Lynn's funding proposal as one might expect. They added it to a long list of action items, subordinate to a number of more pressing problems. It wasn't until the following fiscal year (and budget cycle) that they were able to evaluate it thoroughly. After six months of study, they began to raise serious concerns with Lynn about the viability of competing against entrenched competitors in a complex business where their firm lacked expertise. Another six months passed. The dialogue between Lynn and the CEO deteriorated. Ultimately, two things became crystal clear to all involved: Lynn was a talented professional, and this was a bad business for the firm.

By the time Lynn resigned, the change management episode had consumed three years, generated acrimony and distraction within the firm, and cost the firm $30 million (including severance packages for Lynn and many of her change management colleagues).

The problem in this scenario was neither Lynn nor her entrepreneurial experiment. On the contrary, ambitious professionals with creative ideas *drive* innovation at PSFs. The problem was the linkage between the steering wheel and the tires—the firm and the professionals involved in the change management initiative. Lynn and her colleagues were allowed to drift off course because the firm's leadership wasn't effectively monitoring activities along the perimeter of its business.

Most significant changes occur at the *strategic perimeter* of a firm, the zone where new types of capabilities are developed, new clients are engaged, new markets are penetrated, and experiments are pursued. How the firm's leadership *manages* this strategic perimeter ultimately determines the consequences: costly strategic drift or productive innovation. As we'll see hereafter, to manage the perimeter, leaders must have a firm grasp of the facts and reality of their business, where it is actually headed, on an incremental, quarter-by-quarter basis.

Strategic Identity

One of the great, unanswered questions in professional services, a mystery that transcends sectors and decades, is this: What makes the phone ring? You're sitting at your desk working away, when out of the blue a potential client calls to inquire about your firm's services. You've never met this person, but suddenly you are his new best friend, listening intently to his problems, and hoping that you are his solution. Six weeks later you've sold the business; a couple of years after that he becomes your largest client and one of the most important accounts in the firm.

But why did he call your firm in the first place? Even more perplexing (and disquieting): How many other potential clients decided *not* to call you?

Professional services is inherently a word-of-mouth business. The intangible, personal nature of the services makes it difficult for potential clients to judge the quality or fit of a law firm, an accounting firm, or a consulting firm, so they ask around. When they're not asking, they're listening—to other executives who had such and such an experience with this investment bank or that technology provider. Marketing literature doesn't sway them: Would you hire a lawyer based on a brochure? They want firsthand data, from people with firsthand experience, preferably people whom they know and trust.

Who are the people that have firsthand experience with your firm? Your current employees and existing clients, for certain, but that's only the tip of the iceberg. For every key customer in a client organization (that is, the person who endorses your monthly invoice), there are many—possibly dozens—of other executives at that client who will be happy to proclaim your firm's strengths and weaknesses, often with a vengeance. As for your own employees, they have close friends and family, each of whom also has a point of view about your firm.

In most PSFs, employees turn over at a rate of 10 to 20 percent per year, clients at a rate of 20 to 50 percent per year. Assume that a medium-sized firm grows its business at 10 percent per year for a decade. The consequences are eye popping: At year ten, past clients will outnumber current clients two to one; former employees will also outnumber existing employees. Those numbers are further expanded by colleagues of the firm's prior clients and by friends and family of past firm employees.

Now factor in all the recruits that weren't hired and all the clients who evaluated but didn't hire the firm. If it takes five interviews to land one new hire and three "beauty contests" for each new client, hundreds of additional people have some direct personal knowledge of the firm (and what they will consider a well-informed point of view). By year ten in our simple example, an expanding universe of people have directly or indirectly experienced the firm. They outnumber current clients and employees by almost ten to one.

What do all these people have in common? Each of them has a view of your firm based on personal experience. Some will keep their opinions to themselves; others will spread them around. They may be champions who proclaim your firm's unparalleled excellence, or critics who amplify its shortcomings. Their views may be incomplete, outdated, or unfair—but they are, nevertheless, their views. Indirectly, these are the people who cause your phone to ring—or not—because, in the aggregate, their views create your firm's external strategic identity.

A firm's *external strategic identity* is its cumulative profile in the marketplace: the way the market defines its capabilities, shortfalls, character, and personality. It reflects the market's perceptions of the firm's competitive advantages and disadvantages relative to other service providers ("they are good at IPOs, lousy at M&A"); its target clients ("they're strong with multinationals, relatively weak in Asia"); and its value proposition ("excellent in bringing new companies to market, but very expensive").

Because a firm's external strategic identity lives in the marketplace, outside its bounds, and because it compounds over time (as experience with the firm increases), it is often inconsistent with a firm's self-image, or its internal strategic identity.

The understanding that partners share about their firm's strategy and how it will be accomplished shapes the firm's *internal strategic identity*. It reflects the partners' view of how the firm fits into its competitive environment and of how they, personally, will work to achieve its goals. Internal strategic identity is the firm's genetic code, the deeply held beliefs that drive the partnership toward desired strategic goals.

Since we know Bain & Company well, let's use it as an example. What is Bain's internal strategic identity? Bain partners believe that what distinguishes their firm is providing strategic services to senior executives in a manner that yields extraordinary financial and competitive results for those executives' companies. Consequently, they don't try to offer academic concepts, or sell work to junior planners, or accept engagements with executives they think aren't genuinely committed to getting results. They collaborate with companies and executives over time because they believe collaboration is necessary to produce results. These beliefs go back to the firm's founders, and they are reflected in Bain's mission statement. They influence the way that the firm hires, trains, and promotes its people. They determine the work the firm takes on, the work it says "no" to, the prices it charges, and the clients it pursues and backs away from.

Now contrast Bain with two other outstanding consulting firms, the Boston Consulting Group (BCG) and McKinsey. The three firms are similar in many ways. They recruit from the same pools. They compete against one another for talent and clients. They have some of the same practice areas, work in the same industries, and have offices in many of the same cities throughout the world. They are all private. Nevertheless, their strategic identities, both external and internal, are distinctly different. Bain is about "results," the theme struck by its founders in 1973. BCG is the "intellectual" firm, the one with the brilliant new insights. Bruce Henderson, its founder, was known for writing "Perspectives" on strategy that executives often carried in their pockets. McKinsey partners are "professionals," an identity that goes back to their founder, Marvin Bower, who first envisioned consulting as a profession comparable to the law.

The three investment banks in our study, Goldman Sachs, Alex Brown, and Hambrecht & Quist, provide another vivid example of like businesses with distinct strategic identities. Goldman is a Wall Street firm par excellence: conservative, disciplined, global, and quintessentially blue-chip. Until recently, it was a fiercely private partnership, and membership in the firm is still often referred to as the ultimate brass ring on Wall Street. San Francisco–based H&Q, on the other hand, has more than a whiff of Silicon Valley about it. The pick of the bunch among California investment banks, it sees itself (and is seen) as young, aggressive, and creative—a boutique oriented exclusively around high-growth companies. Alex Brown is similarly identified with high-growth businesses (although in their case, these are more likely to involve health care than microchips). But as you might expect from its longevity (the firm was founded in 1805) and Baltimore roots, its partners relate strongly to the firm's legacy and history.[5]

When there's congruence between a firm's strategic identity (who you think you are) and its external strategic identity (what your experienced constituencies think you do well), the results are terrific. Marakon Associates, a top consulting firm with a rock-solid reputation, illustrates the benefits of such congruence. Marakon coined the phrase and pioneered the practice of "value-based management," and its identity revolves around that focus: maximizing shareholder value for its select client companies. This identity is well understood, internally and externally, and the firm's success over the past twenty years as well as its continued growth today can be largely credited to that fact.

Conversely, when a firm's perceptions of itself are out of sync with its identity in the marketplace, it's a recipe for trouble if not outright failure. CSC Index, the founder and propagator of reengineering, encountered this problem. When CSC's leaders realized that competing consulting firms were effectively selling reengineering services to clients, they decided to move upstream into strategy consulting with the help of new consultants recruited from other firms. CSC Index believed it could enter this new market and command the same respect and following it did in its original area of strength. But potential clients who were deciding to hire a strategy consultant didn't give CSC Index any points for being the masters of reengineering. CSC Index may have thought of itself as a top-tier player, but the marketplace's view of its identity differed, and the firm was unable to attract clients as a strategy provider.

Both internally and externally, a firm's strategic identity develops through experience, not through public relations or marketing or an announced move into a new market segment. Individuals don't change their identities overnight, and neither do professional firms. Strategic identities can and do evolve. But sudden, sharp turns put a firm at risk of an identity crisis, which can ultimately prompt clients and/or stars to seek more compatible relationships. Consider, for example, the consulting firm A.T. Kearney, which was known for logistics and purchasing strategy (and beginning to move aggressively into strategy consulting), when it was sold to EDS. Think about the identity crisis this must have provoked for the partners: There they were, independent professionals, the best in the world at what they did. Suddenly they were part of a big, public, information technology company in Texas, and had gone from being owner/operators to employees in a division. For some that may have been okay. For others, not. But you can't expect professionals to sign up for acquisitions (or alliances or mergers) unless there's a shared perspective on strategic identity—how their firm will be special and different within the new competitive landscape.

How can you know whether your firm's strategic identity is a problem or an asset? The first step is developing an objective awareness of what others who have experienced your firm truly think about you. With such awareness comes the potential to influence those perceptions over time: to reinforce your perceived strengths and neutralize your perceived weaknesses. Firms attack this challenge with all manner of tactics, ranging from alumni gatherings, to surveys of past clients, to interviews of the recruits and clients who reject them. All this takes effort and requires overcoming the natural human tendency to neither seek nor accept negative feedback. Yet awareness is half the battle: The best PSFs understand the need to understand.

Strategic Shortcuts

Most professionals are inherently hurried, impatient people. Typically ambitious, type A personalities, they work in a world of client deadlines and personal productivity, where everything was due yesterday, and where good enough never is.

Professionals like shortcuts because shortcuts save time. Whether it's a shorter route to the airport or a more effective administrative system, their hardwired orientation is to free up as much precious time as possible for current and potential clients. Normally, this behavior is appropriate. It encourages higher firm utilization (and thereby improved profitability and personal income) and reflects the can-do approach required to win every day in the competitive arena. When it comes to strategic choices, however, shortcuts—though an alluring prospect—also represent an enormous risk.

In recent years, PSFs have pursued a panoply of bold strokes in the hopes of redefining their industries and gaining sustainable competitive advantage (or at least competitive parity). As we saw in chapter 1, there have been mergers and acquisitions, joint ventures, and spin-offs. Mergers are rationalized on the grounds of *synergy:* the idea that two good firms, added together, will make one great firm, which can better serve clients. Acquisitions, aside from enriching the sellers, promise the buyers access to new markets. The merger of Price Waterhouse and Coopers & Lybrand may have been a brilliant strategic move in a rapidly consolidating industry; likewise, H&Q's decision to sell itself to Chase. But it will probably be ten years before anyone knows for sure.

Why so long? Because the internal logic of the PSF business model means that the ultimate result of any strategic bold stroke depends on the subsequent behavior of individual stars. Achieving synergy among disparate PSFs is not like consolidating two chains of retail stores. It's more like moving in with the new family across the street.

Rather than lending themselves to one-off bold strokes, PSFs' strategies more often resemble long marches, in which greatness is achieved client by client, star by star, day by day. Even bold-stroke strategies are actually long marches in disguise: Just ask the partners of PricewaterhouseCoopers as they try to integrate two complex, multicultural, and multinational organizations. Building a successful PSF is akin to building a brick wall: You may want to add many bricks at once, but it's tough to do so without toppling the wall. Put simply, there are few (if any) rapid paths to enduring greatness.

Organizational Characteristics: The Key to Achieving Strategic Goals

Strategy is about winning in the marketplace. Winning is especially tough in the dynamic professional services marketplace where stars drive a firm's strategic decisions as well as the implementation of those decisions. How do outstanding firms achieve their strategic goals, given all the inherent tensions, complexities, and risks we've been discussing? How do they guide the behavior of multiple generations of professionals, year after year, such that people consistently do what's right for the firm?

The answer lies in a handful of organizational characteristics and the choices firms make about them. When these organizational characteristics are aligned with the needs of the stars and the strategy of the firm, they create the conditions under which the strategy can be implemented effectively. Because they evolve over time, through the cumulative choices a firm's leadership makes to shape the behavior of its stars and their relationships, they cannot easily be replicated. Because this is the case, they can create a formidable competitive barrier. A competitor may copy your firm's goals, but cannot easily duplicate your means of achieving them.

The organizational characteristics that promote (or undermine) a firm's efforts to implement its strategy take shape along three separate but related dimensions: its organization, its culture, and its leadership. *Organization* encompasses the firm's people systems, structure, and governance. *Culture* deals with the underlying core of beliefs and values, which shapes behavior within the firm in so many subtle ways. *Leadership* reflects both the formal leadership responsibilities attached to specific roles (such as chief executive, office head, or practice leader) and the personal leadership that can be provided by every partner-level professional every day. These dimensions and their relationship to firm strategy are illustrated in figure 3-4, the "Alignment Pyramid." (This figure will reappear in chapters 4 through 8, as we focus on each of the dimensions in turn and in detail.)

One aspect of "means" that is missing from this pyramid deserves mention here. This is the functional support staff that leverage the firm's professional staff, improving both productivity and service quality. While the mix and magnitude of departments may vary across firms and industries, a few are consistently critical. Information technology

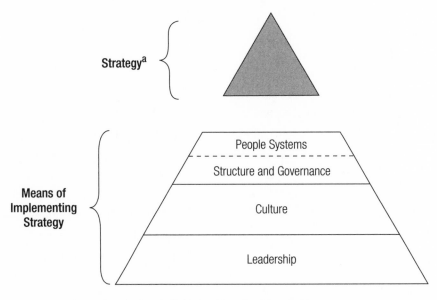

Strategy[a]

Means of Implementing Strategy

People Systems

Structure and Governance

Culture

Leadership

[a]See figure 3-1, "Strategy Pyramid," for a detailed look at this portion of the pyramid.

Figure 3-4 **Alignment Pyramid**

(which is *the* client value proposition for IT consulting firms, of course) has become the backbone of most PSFs, from communication systems to productivity tools. Knowledge management, too, is especially important as the scale and complexity of firms increase (and it, too, is a "product" for many firms). Finance, always critical, becomes a highly strategic issue if a firm is considering changes to its balance sheet or ownership structure (such as an IPO). Marketing is playing a far more prominent role among even the most understated professional firms. Human resource professionals provide the administrative foundation for many aspects of people systems, governance, and leadership. Taken together, these functions (and others depending on the nature of a particular organization) can have an enormous impact on a firm's ability to achieve its strategic goals.

Proprietary strategy and sustainable competitive advantage are the two holy grails of business. While these are enticing concepts, achieving either is rare indeed. Barring patent protection or monopolistic power, most strategies can eventually be copied, and most competitive advantages are temporary at best. The capitalist system thrives on creative destruction: the chaotic process whereby competitive dynamics overthrow successful enterprises.

Professional service firms are no exception to this economic fact of life. Embedded in their business model, however, are the seeds of powerful competitive advantages, which can approach some level of sustainability. Because people are different, firms are different. Because groups of people behave differently, no two organizations are exactly alike. In these businesses, both financial success and sustainability rely on outstanding individuals, their client relationships, and their behavior toward their firm. The result is a complex system of components, which is fragile and vulnerable, but which can also be exceptionally powerful and enduring. It is no coincidence that the average age of the eighteen companies we studied is seventy years.

The ability to create an aligned and proprietary professional service business rests on the ability to attract, retain, and motivate multiple generations of stars. It is that topic to which we now turn.

4 ★ Turning Talent into Stars

The Enduring Edge

SITTING IN *the executive conference room, Kate and Grant, senior vice presidents at a global manufacturing company, reflected on the bake-off between two information technology providers that had just ended. The firms had been vying for a six-month contract with their company, and at the outset the decision had looked like a no-brainer.*

"Right up until this morning, I was sure we'd hire Atlas," Grant said. *"They're bigger, they have more experience, and their reputation is much more prestigious. When the senior partner made his final pitch, he really stole the show. But then I thought about the fact that we might never see that particular partner again. So after the meeting broke up, I made a point of*

talking informally with the junior consultants and associates on the project team. I did the same thing with the folks from Technova, and bottom line, the team from Atlas looked like the second string compared to them."

"I think we all felt that way," agreed Kate. "The senior partner at Atlas is clearly outstanding. If we were hiring him alone to do the job, there'd be no question about my vote. But the younger consultants at Technova seem more talented, more motivated, and much better able to relate to our style and needs. And they're the ones who are going to work with us every day and drive the quality of the work."

"Six months and $3 million," mused Grant, shaking his head. "And the people at Atlas will wonder why they didn't get the job. I'll call them tomorrow with the bad news. I'll keep it brief, though; no reason to burn bridges."

For every winner there are many losers. Second place is no place in the competition among PSFs.

Among professionals *rainmaker* is a universally understood honorific referring to exceptional salespeople who develop strong and profitable client relationships. Successful firms nurture and develop rainmaking capability through performance reviews, compensation systems, and promotion criteria. Rainmakers are praised as the kings and queens of organizations, fueling growth and competitive success. Firms rich in rainmakers generally succeed—at least for a while.

But there's another core competency that is *more* important than rainmaking to a firm's long-term success: *starmaking* (which is an integral part of the firm's people systems. See figure 4-1). Starmaking is an organization's competency at attracting, retaining, developing, and motivating star talent—the future professionals and leaders who build the firm from generation to generation. Just as there are individual rainmakers, there are partners who become starmakers—people especially adept at building star capacity within a firm. They, and the starmaking firms they work for, understand *the* basic fact of life in professional services: *The people you pay are more important over time than the people who pay you.*

Why? Talent is a professional firm's only sustainable source of competitive advantage. If you look at a great firm and ask, "Which came first, the star or the client?" the star came first every time. Professional organizations achieve and maintain greatness by attracting and retaining stars who attract and retain clients and, in turn, more new stars.

What does all this mean to you? The key to your firm's continuing competitive success is building star talent. Not landing the biggest clients—clients can be stolen. Not coming up with a best-selling book or proprietary process—intellectual property can be copied. Not being the first mover in a new geographic area—competitors can open more offices, too. None of these advantages is sustainable. Star talent is. It is what can create a firm's enduring competitive edge!

Building this talent begins with the competition for stars, which has seldom been fiercer. As more and more businesses discover that they have to compete on brains, demand is exploding for the kind of skills and capabilities that power PSFs. In fact, we'd be willing to bet that in the time it takes you to read this book (if not this chapter) three things will happen: (1) One of your key clients (someone whose business you can't afford to lose) will have dinner with a partner from a rival firm; (2) a star recruit (someone you would love to

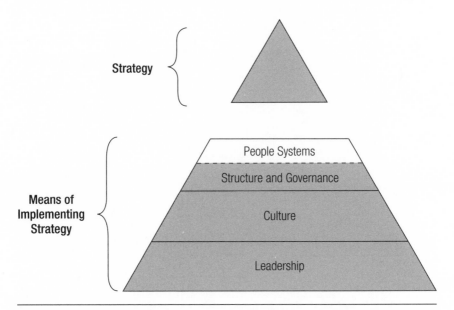

Figure 4-1   Alignment Pyramid: People Systems—Talent to Stars

hire, possibly someone neither you nor any of your partners has ever met) will decide not to pursue an opportunity with your firm; and (3) one of your star employees (a future partner or senior executive in the making) will accept another job or think seriously about doing so.

Virtually every competent professional knows how to handle the first scenario. Good firms have well-developed systems in place to help them understand and respond to clients' needs. They monitor client behavior religiously, and the moment the backlog falls, or retention dips, or a client flirts with another firm, the partners swing into action. The senior partner, for example, might fly out to the client site she hasn't visited in a few weeks to see how her team is working with the CEO that awarded her firm the project. Or she might make an extra effort to solicit feedback from the client or to let the client know how the project is progressing. She might also have dinner with a client that has given the firm repeat business to ask candidly how she and her partners have been doing at meeting the client's needs and expectations.

The second and third scenarios are another matter, however. At most firms, desirable recruits who don't sign on and young associates who jump ship are seen as facts of life. "These things happen," people say, "and we're a big firm with lots of employees."

In great firms, however, the senior people worry as much about missing out on or losing new talent as they do about missing out on or losing good clients. And they go to equally great lengths to prevent those events from occurring. Seasoned professionals devote time and attention to activities such as recruiting and performance reviews, which many lesser firms neglect or delegate to human resource departments. A senior partner, for example, might spend several days each month to aid his firm's recruiting efforts. Or he might take a young colleague to lunch between client meetings to ask her how things are going on her current assignment. Everyone in the firm believes that these activities represent critical long-term investments, and, as a result, the firm's habitual practices for developing its new talent are as systematic and as strategically aligned as its practices for developing new business opportunities.

Marketplace of Stars

Before we delve into the ways outstanding firms attract, retain, develop, and motivate their new talent, let's first revisit what we mean by *star*. The fact that you picked up this book suggests you're already hiring talented individuals. Probably most of them are great human beings as well. But not all of these great people are destined to be stars as we're using the term.

Stars are people who have the highest *future* value for the firm, the individuals who will have the most impact on the business in the years ahead. Most, but not all, partner-level professionals are stars, as are potential partners and other exceptional performers who fill critical roles in the organization. They are stars both because of their professional abilities and because they put the firm first. Prima donnas need not apply. By definition, therefore, stars are always a subset of a firm's recruits and its young professionals. Ultimately, stars constitute the firm's leadership and the best of its professional talent. They reinforce its strategic identity day by day, as they deliver services to clients and develop less-experienced professionals. In other words, they are the core group who will drive the firm's destiny in the longer term.

Consider the following three people:

- This woman began her career with Ogilvy & Mather in 1971 as an account executive just three years after graduating from Smith College and one year after receiving her M.B.A. from Columbia University. (During the time between graduate school and Ogilvy, she worked as a product manager for Clairol.) At Ogilvy, she worked on a broad range of accounts, including Clairol, American Express, Pepsi, and Campbell. In 1980, she was named group director for the American Express account, gaining her first experience with direct marketing. Six years later, she moved to Ogilvy & Mather Direct and her first senior management job as general manager of the New York office. She became president of Ogilvy & Mather Direct in 1989. In 1991, she returned to Ogilvy & Mather Advertising as president of the New York office.

- This man joined Skadden Arps after receiving his degree from the University of Pennsylvania Law School in 1969. He made partner in 1978. Founding and heading the Financial Institutions Merger & Acquisitions Group is one of his many contributions to the firm. Today he is known as one of the world's leading banking lawyers. He has represented leading financial institutions in acquisition transactions and has served as counsel in landmark cases.

- This man, also a graduate of the University of Pennsylvania, started his career with Ernst & Young in 1961. He earned his C.P.A. and progressed through the ranks of the firm's audit practice, making partner in 1971. In 1981, he was named managing partner of the New York office. Four years later, he became vice chairman and managing partner of the New York region and a member of the firm's management committee.

Who are these people? Respectively, Shelly Lazarus, Robert Sheehan, and Philip Laskawy. Lazarus was named CEO of Ogilvy & Mather Worldwide in 1996, twenty-five years after beginning her career with the firm. She became its chairman at the end of 1997. Sheehan was selected as Skadden Arps's executive partner in 1993. And Laskawy became chairman and CEO of Ernst & Young in 1994, and chairman of Ernst & Young International in 1997.

These stars' histories are revealing. They and most of their counterparts at other outstanding firms are "homegrown" professionals who have had long and broad experience with their firms. They are great at what they do and, more important, have the respect of their peers and of the professionals coming up the ranks behind them. By virtue of having succeeded within their organizations, they both understand and embody the values of their firms and serve as teachers and inspiration to future generations of leaders.

The obvious question? How to identify stars like Lazarus, Sheehan, and Laskawy early on. The answer? You can't do so with certainty. The hotshot at the head of the class on day one may be overtaken and left behind by a self-starter with a less prestigious pedigree.

The analyst who starts out like a rocket may lose altitude, when she has to manage projects or client relationships. The hard-driving associate your clients love may decide he wants more from life than catching another airplane. Even in the firms that are most successful at recruiting and developing high-performing professionals, predicting who will succeed—and stick—is at best a batting-average proposition.

Unfortunately, however, this doesn't let you off the hook. Despite all the variables you cannot control, you have to identify stars early and often, as best you can. A critical indicator is the feedback you'll begin to receive almost immediately from the marketplaces in which your new professionals personally compete. There are two. The first is the *internal* market for staffing, which is triggered by the firm's ongoing need to decide whom to assign where. The second is the *external* market generated by client demands.

We'll examine the internal market first. Unlike most businesses, people in PSFs begin to compete with one another early in their careers. That's the way the economics of PSFs work.

Remember that the fortunes of any firm ultimately turn on its ability to sell as much of its professionals' time as fully (utilization) and at as high a price as possible year after year. Well, that same principle applies to individuals. (The utilization of individual professionals, in aggregate, becomes firmwide utilization.) When lots of partners are clamoring for one associate, while another is left sitting on the bench, the invisible hand of the internal market is telling you something about their perceived relative value. Additional feedback comes, a little later on in a young professional's career, when clients are willing to say not only "I like Jill" but also "I like her well enough to buy more of her time." Associates who are highly utilized are moving ahead in the firm. They are your current set of young stars.

Most professionals understand the internal marketplace intuitively. And in any PSF worth its salt, any office manager will be able to tell you a year after a new crop of recruits has been hired who among them is in the top quartile and who is in the bottom. Indeed, all of the outstanding firms we know have a formal process in place to help them identify internal stars.

Bain, for example, ranks all of its professionals worldwide every six months as part of its overall performance management system. Ernst & Young uses the cumulative information from quarterly evaluations, evaluations from individual engagements, and round tables to do a forced distribution ranking on a scale of 1 to 5 with 5 being the highest each year. (Because no one ever gets a 1, the scale is effectively 2 to 5. If you have a 2 ranking, you will most likely be eased out.)

Latham & Watkins's performance review process is worth looking at in some detail because it is consistently careful and thorough and also because it is inclusive, giving associates the opportunity to influence important decisions and the acknowledgment that their voices matter to their senior colleagues. Twice a year, the law firm conducts performance reviews for each associate. The data come from every partner and senior associate the associate has worked with. The firm's Associates Committee divides the associates being evaluated (close to 700 in all) into groups of twenty-five or thirty, with one committee member taking responsibility for each group. That person then looks over each file in his or her group, reads all the reviewers' comments, analyzes strengths and weaknesses, and writes a brief performance message. Then the committee meets for five or six intense days to discuss the performance messages for each of the 700 associates and to reach agreement on the feedback each will be given. For associates in their seventh year, the feedback includes an "on track" call that lets them know whether they are on track to become a partner.

Latham's process is unusual in that it involves associates as members of the Associates Committee; however, it shares two important benefits with the reviews that go on at all the firms we studied. It enables senior people to keep track of junior people and to identify the top performers who are most likely to become stars of the firm, and it enables junior people to understand where they are in their careers and how they are doing relative to their internal cohort.

Now let's examine the external market. As we've said, stars are not only defined in relation to their peers within a firm but also in relation to their counterparts in other firms. Though this may seem obvious, the external marketplace can be dangerously easy to overlook for several reasons. First, it is extremely difficult (if not impossible) to get the data necessary to make a comparison between individuals at different firms. Second, professionals most often think of the quality of a firm as a whole, rather than the quality of individuals within that firm; it's often hard to unbundle individuals from the firm overall. Finally, people naturally like to think highly of their own firms and shy away from criticizing themselves as compared to competitors.

And yet it is critical to acknowledge and evaluate how the external market views your talent. One way to do this is through interviews with clients, both those you work for and those you've lost to other firms. Ask them why they chose you or why they went to a competitor and you're likely to hear something about the relative quality of your professionals. Another way to assess the external marketplace is to consistently gather facts about your firm's recruiting performance:

- What is your recruiting yield compared to competitors—especially for the most attractive recruits?

- Why do you win? And what is the root cause of your failures?

- Are you even interviewing the best people? What about potential stars who didn't apply to your firm (but did apply to your competition)?

- Which sources of recruits offer your firm the richest supply of potential stars, and how well do you subsequently retain them?

- Which sources of recruits are high-cost and which are low-cost, including all the professional time involved?

By analyzing such facts over time, you will be able to improve your overall performance at attracting potential stars.

Among information technology consulting firms, IBM Consulting has a reputation for recruiting and developing outstanding professionals relative to its competitors. If you were to randomly select a sample of the people at IBM and one of its competitors, on average you'd find better people at IBM. And like the interest on financial investments, the returns on talent are compounded over time. The external marketplace is critically important. Great firms win because, relative to their competitors, they consistently play with the first string, and everyone in the marketplace knows it.

Investing in Stars—Neither Free nor Easy

As co-head of investment banking at Goldman Sachs, Rob Kaplan has a lot on his mind—multimillion-dollar deals, the deployment of his colleagues to various projects. Prominent among his concerns is the progress of the new associates in his department. "If someone isn't doing well," he told us, "I get very actively involved as early as possible, because sometimes . . . there are things that can be done to get them to improve. We've seen that a lot. . . . I'll sit down with the person and talk about what he or she needs to focus on. Then we might team them up with another senior person, [or] move them to a different job. For instance, some people are very talented, but they're shy, and so the best thing may be to move them into an industry group where they can become experts and gain confidence."

Kaplan's comments reflect his and Goldman's commitment to developing its young talent, but they are not unique to this firm: they are representative of what we heard from the leadership of Latham & Watkins, Korn/Ferry, Ernst & Young, and Young & Rubicam, to name a few. Enduring firms such as these make huge investments in their young professionals.

Money is the easy part. Offering recruits compensation that meets or exceeds the market for their profession and level is standard operating procedure in most good firms. The transparency and reach of the market for talent were amply illustrated in the fall of 2000, when compensation for young associates at leading U.S. law firms jumped as much as 50 percent almost overnight in response to new offers made by Silicon Valley firms who found themselves losing talent to dot-com start-ups. More complicated—and less common—are the investments firms make when star producers and leaders, like Kaplan, allocate time to recruiting and developing new associates. For young stars, the time of partners and senior people is the most valuable currency. When Alan Levenson, senior partner at Fulbright & Jaworski, lets associates know what he thinks of their work (which he does right away, in real time, when he works with them), he is not only teaching them how to do things "the Fulbright & Jaworski way," he's also showing them that he cares about their progress and is interested in them as individuals.

Cristina Morgan, managing director at Hambrecht & Quist and codirector of investment banking, sends that same message when she lets her young associates know how good (or how poor) their work was on any given project. "You never walk out of a meeting and say, 'OK, so what?'" she told us. "You walk out of a meeting and say 'This data was flawed. Here's why it was wrong. That was an embarrassing moment for Hambrecht & Quist. That doesn't work. Never do that again.' Or, 'I cannot believe that you pulled this book together inside of twenty-four hours with no notice, and not knowing anything about this industry. You are a genius. How did you do it?'" By taking the time to go over the day's events, Morgan is not only prepping her associates for the "next round," she's also showing them that she is genuinely, personally, concerned with their progress.

What makes these investments challenging is that clients want partner time, too. They not only want it, they demand it, and they're willing to pay for it. So when a firm chooses to allocate its most valuable resources away from clients and to young stars, the economic consequences are real and visible. Utilization, and therefore profitability, will decline in the short term. Short-term revenue is explicitly sacrificed to build toward longer-term success (and, of course, subsequent revenue). If you factor in the odds of any given associate making it to partner (or managing director or senior vice president), the rationale for making substantial investments in young talent looks even shakier.

Why, then, do great firms invest so heavily in stars? To put it bluntly, they understand the costs of mediocrity.

The Costs of Mediocrity

When we say *mediocrity,* we're not referring to incompetence. We'd be astonished if anyone reading this book were hiring people they thought couldn't perform. By mediocrity, we mean the cost of employing people who are *less talented than those who built your firm and/or are now leading it*. The economic consequences of mediocrity show up more slowly than the economic consequences of fewer billable hours. But ultimately the price tag is even higher because these costs are measured longer-term in deteriorating assets and weakened competitive position.

The logic is simple and insidious. Suppose, for example, that a firm has a string of bad recruiting years and ends up hiring B players instead of the A players it has traditionally attracted. At first, clients won't notice any difference because the newcomers will be working on teams that are still dominated by A players. Over time, however, the B players will have to manage client work themselves. What happens then? At best, dissatisfied clients will complain, and the partners will be able to reassign people to accommodate them. At worst, clients deliver the bad news by taking their business elsewhere.

If the story stopped there, it would be costly enough. But it doesn't, because by now the B players will also have a role in developing new recruits. And young stars don't like working for less-talented bosses any more than key clients like being served by less-talented professionals. They may put up with it for a little while (although the days when a firm could count on its recruits to "grin and bear it" are gone and unlikely to recur, whatever the state of the economy). But they won't stick around indefinitely.

We can think of a number of CEOs who were once frustrated professionals working under less-talented or uninspiring people, who left their firms and founded their own companies with a stated commitment to quality professionals. And several professionals at one of the firms we researched told us that the opportunity to work under excellent people on challenging projects was one of the key reasons they had left prior jobs to join this firm. So even if a firm has begun attracting A players again, it will have trouble holding onto them unless it is prepared to do some serious pruning among its now more-senior people, who are B players.

This story has many versions. One of the most common involves superstar founders whose supersized egos drive out everyone below them except the people who have no other options. Whatever the particulars, the effects are the same. A small marginal difference in the quality of people coming into a firm at any given moment will have order-of-magnitude effects five, ten, or twenty years down the line.

Given this logic, investing in young talent looks like a no-brainer. Yet many intelligent professionals and firms don't do it. Why? Agreeing with this idea in principle and putting it into practice are very different things.

The Hidden Bias against Investing

You're running an office, and you and your management team decide it's time to commit to paying more attention to recruiting and developing young stars. To give the idea some teeth, your management team follows up by budgeting 20 percent of partner time to talent-related activities. All the partners signal their assent.

That's on Monday. What happens Tuesday? On Tuesday, a client calls and partner X says, "I know I'm supposed to do a performance review today, but I can't get to it." On Wednesday, the client calls again. "Sorry, I can't go to campus and do that recruiting." On Thursday, the partner is traveling. Partner Y is in the middle of selling the biggest client she's ever dealt with; she, too, puts off her performance reviews, her campus recruiting. You are dismayed, but at the same time, your most important client is having a meltdown, and you've got to push everything on your own agenda aside to handle the crisis. Never mind a few lunches with young associates; you've canceled a family vacation.

No PSF is exempt from this struggle. Even in the organizations that do the best job of balancing star development and client demands, the pressure never lets up.

What's different about enduring firms is that they systematically reinforce their partners' willingness to develop younger colleagues; in doing so, they breed starmakers. At Young & Rubicam, for example, you no longer can get a bonus if you don't do a self-evaluation and performance appraisals of the people who work with you. At Bain, one of the five criteria used to determine compensation is "people asset building," which includes mentoring, coaching, and developing others within the case-team setting and outside it. Mentoring, coaching, and recruiting are also on the list of qualitative criteria used to evaluate partner performance at Goldman Sachs.

Senior partners at most firms agree that even with systemic reinforcement, it's challenging to devote the necessary time to developing stars. As John Dowell, a partner at McKinsey, explained, "The real learning here takes place with the client on engagement teams. You'll have one to two partners and three to five associates, say, who are together for six months. So, the real development challenge is to make sure that in fact, the partners in those engagements are spending adequate amounts of time with their teams. But there are all kinds of pressures, as you get bigger, particularly, that tend to take the partners away from that."

Gus Blackshear, managing partner at Fulbright & Jaworski, identified one of the principal challenges, when he told us, rather ruefully, "You get to praise people, which I enjoy doing very much, and you also have to be candid when they're falling short of what they should be doing, and that's sometimes not a very pleasant thing. I think some days it would be largely more rewarding to represent clients, have them appreciate what you've done for them, send them a bill, and get paid."

Absent some kind of systemic reinforcement, most senior professionals are likely to follow the temptation to consistently put clients' needs ahead of starmaking. Why? There are the day-to-day pressures clients exert. And there are the tangible rewards and praise that come from meeting client needs.

Professional service firms' incentives tip toward clients because PSFs are top-line driven; their short-term financials hinge on revenue generation and utilization. Therefore the natural orientation is to recognize and reward rainmaking above all else.

The great and enduring firms, however, understand that rainmaking alone is inadequate. They know that over time starmaking is more important than rainmaking and that, in fact, the latter is entirely dependent on the former. They've witnessed one-generation firms, founded by a handful of rainmakers, that fell apart when those rainmakers failed to replicate themselves—when they failed at starmaking. Enduring PSFs recognize the pressures against investing in starmaking, so they design their people systems to reinforce starmaking as well as rainmaking. They recognize individuals who are "culture carriers" (Goldman Sachs) or "people asset builders" (Bain). They also respect the commitment it represents. At Latham & Watkins, the chair of the Associates Committee is seen as a prime candidate to become the next managing partner. These firms rebalance their organizations' overall incentives to develop people as well as clients.

What Do Star Recruits Want?

You can't invest in stars you haven't been able to hire. To compete for stars, you have to look more attractive—and stay more attractive—than other available options. Compensation and benefits are a piece of a firm's value proposition, but they are table stakes. What's crucial is your ability to meet the needs of your young stars as *they* define them.

Think about all the time and attention you regularly give clients, the people who pay you: the networking, the interviews with potential clients to understand their needs, the endless meetings with current clients to make sure you know what's on their minds. You know that if a firm doesn't understand—and satisfy—client needs, it will quickly go out of business. Remember the Internet companies that had such great potential and crashed? Chances are that many of them weren't address-ing client needs as well as more established bricks-and-mortar counter-parts, or they were unable to keep pace as their clients' needs evolved.

Now think about the "clients" you pay, the potential stars who are the future foundation of your firm. How much do you truly under-stand their needs? When was the last time you took a young associate to dinner to learn more about what was on his mind? Even during the halcyon days of Digitas's growth, for David Kenny, the CEO, it was every month.

When was the last time you solicited honest feedback from some-one leaving the firm as you would routinely from a client who decided to take his business elsewhere? Or asked a star recruit what motivated her to go work for your competitors rather than you? When you talk to your people, you may find out that the professional you just lost to a competitor left because she needed to be in Cleveland and you don't have an office there. Or you may learn that she felt like she didn't fit in with her cohort at your firm. You may discover that Sarah felt underutilized and bored, or that the pressures of the job and the long hours were too much for her. You may be surprised to hear that Rick wants more formal training or that José left the firm because of the reputation it had among important people in the industry, and he was afraid of closing doors on his future career. It can be hard to understand the needs of the people you pay because they have little incentive to tell you. But clients don't always have much incentive either, and most experienced professionals become adept at teasing out the information they need. The issue is applying the same skill—and time—to your stars in the making.

While young professionals will have their own particular needs, there are some things we can generalize about. First, they want to learn. They have been learning all their lives, they're good at it, and they like it. In addition, they know that learning increases their market value. They join one firm rather than another because they think it will be worth more to them to work there, so the education they value—and that you must provide—has to be practical and it has to be marketable.

Second, they want career options. People joining PSFs today want to use them as a stepping-stone to something else. They're not thinking about their first job as an end point, a destination. It's just the next phase in their career, and they might go through many phases. The average M.B.A. typically stays at a first job for two to three years at most. Lawyers used to join firms and stay for decades, if not their entire career. So did accountants. Not now. The rate of mobility across professions and across firms has increased dramatically. This means that young stars are thinking about whether your organization will open future doors or close them. The doors can be inside the firm or outside it. The key question is, "What are you going to do to help me continue to develop and make me more marketable in the years ahead?"

Third, most young professionals value affiliation and teamwork. If they were pure entrepreneurs, they'd likely take a different path than the one PSFs offer. Young stars want to be affiliated with like-minded professionals, and this affiliation contributes to the energy that drives them. They also like to serve, and to feel as though they are making a difference with their work. They need to feel emotionally connected to their firm—to know that senior people (at least some) really *care* about them and their success.

At the same time, they also value the autonomy of professional work—the chance to clear their own patch of the woods. At a law firm, this freedom might mean getting a chance to research a type of case or practice area that the firm's senior people don't have expertise in. At an advertising firm, it might be a senior leader letting you run with a design for a new ad. Young professionals are independent minded and want to have a voice in matters that affect them, like which projects they work on and which ones they don't.

Finally, some young professionals value flexibility that enables them to better balance their professional and personal lives; this desire for flexibility may become more important over time. One partner at a consulting firm who had three kids at home was relieved when her firm allowed her to work part-time and from home, changing her role slightly, without making her feel as though she would no longer be a valuable asset. As a result of the firm's support, she remained as committed as she always had been rather than drifting away from the firm and eventually leaving. She worked part-time for over ten years, and at age fifty was still happily employed by the firm and still adding value.

At this point, you're probably nodding your head in recognition of the breed. You're probably also saying, "Wait a minute, it sounds as though you think we should put the monkeys in charge of the zoo. Why shouldn't these kids pay their dues the same way the rest of us did when we started out?"

They should. Of course they should. It goes almost without saying that your firm is going to demand a lot from its recruits. They know there's no free lunch, that you'll expect them to work hard and long, to meet escalating performance standards, and, over time, to generate knowledge, build client relationships, and develop new young stars.

They know that you expect them to throw themselves into the firm, to strive to be part of the team for the long term. But going forward, you and your partners have to make your side of the deal explicit and follow through on it. Otherwise you're likely to find that your stars aren't sticking around to meet your standards because their needs aren't being met. The inertia in the system that used to work in a firm's favor has diminished if not disappeared. Today, the value proposition between you and your recruits not only has to be a two-way street, it must also be continually updated. Yesterday's best practices will not ensure tomorrow's success.

You Will Become Who You Hire

Every experienced professional knows that all clients are not created equal. For some clients your firm isn't the right provider and never will be. For others you're a natural, and, in their case, once a relationship is forged, it typically deepens and strengthens over the years. The same principle applies to employees. The challenge is to be as smart about identifying, attracting, and retaining star talent as you are about finding and working with key clients.

Because PSFs understand the client-side economics, they routinely target certain customers, in certain marketplaces, with certain value propositions (the activities that usually go under the rubric of marketing and business development). Great recruiters bring a similarly strategic mindset to the hiring process. They identify the skills, preparation, and attitude people need to contribute to the firm's success. They identify where the people who possess those attributes are likely to be found. Then they pursue those people vigorously because they know that if the recruiting isn't right, even the best developmental efforts will come to naught.

Firms that consistently succeed in starmaking invariably target certain universities, industries, or competitors where their yield historically has been good. But they rarely limit themselves to sources that have worked before. Great recruiters are imaginative as well as energetic. Young & Rubicam, for example, once recruited artists in Poland right off the street while they were creating their art. The details? On one side of a racetrack just outside Warsaw stands a 2.5-kilometer-long wall that has become a canvas for the country's graffiti artists. Each night, up to fifteen artists show up to create their art. One night, a group of Young & Rubicam recruiters arrived at the wall before dark, hid behind trees, and waited for the artists to show up and start painting. When they did, the advertising folks jumped out from their hiding places and offered jobs to several whose work they liked.

Sharp recruiters also avoid being blindsided by snobbery into thinking that anyone from a blue-chip school will outperform everyone from anywhere else. New York law firm Skadden Arps could doubtless fill its recruiting class solely from top-ten schools, but as Robert Sheehan, its managing partner, explained, "Hiring is very competitive because the major firms have become bigger, but the law schools have not. We might take two or three people each year at Brooklyn Law School, because if they are in the top 10 percent of students, they have shown a record of achievement which makes us think they have the brain power to be the kind of lawyer that we like to see."

Perhaps most important, at every outstanding firm we studied, firm leaders are heavily involved in recruitment. Of course they leverage their time, by using young associates to do the preliminary rounds of interviewing or employing human resource specialists to help with scheduling, coordination, and advice. But once the serious candidates are identified, more experienced leaders invariably become deeply engaged.

This is particularly true for search firms: Because they hire only experienced people, their recruiting processes are exceptionally rigorous. But they illustrate the care and attention devoted to hiring we found among leading firms. At Heidrick & Struggles, for example, individuals who are brought into the firm have to go through a recruiting process that CEO Patrick Pittard says the firm would *never* recommend to its clients. The recruit must have the sponsorship of the office he is being recruited into, and he must have met every director in that office as well as the practice management partner and others from the specific practice interested in him. He must also meet at least five members of the firm's executive committee. Daunting? Absolutely. But as a result of this rigorous process, Heidrick & Struggles has excelled in selecting people who will succeed and stay with the firm for a long time. "The process is awful," Pittard told us. "But we don't make many mistakes."

When we asked firms why their leaders were so involved in recruiting activities, we were given several explanations. Partners are credible and persuasive in convincing prospects to join the firm. Their experience enables them to identify candidates who have the right set of skills and to whom the firm's value proposition will appeal. Involvement in recruiting means that they will be more likely to commit to developing the young stars who join the firm. All are valid reasons. But there is another reason, which was evident if not always expressed: Experienced leaders who have grown up in a firm are great culture carriers. They have a sixth sense about their firm's strategic identity. So they are particularly well equipped to recognize potential recruits who are most likely to "fit." (The primary function of many professional firms' Web sites, by the way, is to present the firm and help potential recruits figure out from *their* perspective whether they'd be a good fit.) The fit we're talking about here, and that great recruiters search for, revolves around values, ambitions, and dreams—qualities it's impossible to measure or quantify.

Bain's chief executive, John Donahoe, puts it this way. "How would you feel about spending a few days on the road with this particular guy or gal?" "How would you feel about having dinner with this person?" "Would they fit in with our culture, which generally is energetic, not very hierarchical, meritocratic, collaborative, results-oriented? How would this person function in our environment?"

At Goldman Sachs, "We're looking for people who have a history of accomplishment, yes, but we're also looking for people we think are capable of working within our system," Rob Kaplan explained. "For example, some people [who interview with the firm] are brilliant, but they are not communicators; it's evident that they really don't want to work with other people; we'd be hesitant in those cases."

And Bruce Lupatkin, director of research at Hambrecht & Quist, put it this way: "We tend to self-select for people who want to work in a more collegial environment. Our business breeds big egos, but we go out of our way to try to avoid that. It's rare, for example, that we'll play in what I call the 'free agent draft' when we need to hire somebody. And it would be very unusual for us to go and cherry-pick a hotshot from another Wall Street firm. Our hiring practice is really consistent with the overall culture of the place; we're very collegial."

Hambrecht & Quist's Cristina Morgan told us that she knows within ten minutes of meeting a recruit whether they're the right "fit" for the firm. "If you love small, innovative technology or health care companies, there is no better place to work on the planet because you work with a bunch of other people who are crazy about these technologies. You *won't* be working with a bunch of people who are saying, 'Gee, I did six more deals than you did this year, and I'm cooler.' "

One of the biggest mistakes a firm can make is to persuade a candidate to join when there isn't a good fit between her aspirations and the firm's. The reason is that you have to deliver on your value proposition. If that's not aligned with the recruit's needs, neither she nor the firm will benefit and thrive. You can't develop stars you haven't recruited, but most of the heavy lifting takes place after they've accepted the job, when you begin the development process that will help them become your firm's future stars.

Working to Learn, Learning to Work

Developing a star recruit into a seasoned star is a multiyear journey. But unlike travels with clients, these journeys have few signposts. Clients let you know how you're doing every month when you send them a bill. But there's no way to know, quarter by quarter, which of your young stars are actively looking for new jobs. You know they all get calls and e-mails from recruiters and friends. Are they returning them? You'll never be sure.

So how do you guard against losing your stars? It's not easy, after all, to satisfy clients who want everything yesterday and employees who don't want 24/7 work lives. Or to reconcile a recruit's need to learn with a client's preference for someone experienced. How can you maintain an environment that will motivate talented youngsters while simultaneously giving your clients what they want?

Resolving this conundrum begins with the work itself. The work that young professionals do *is* the world they inhabit, what motivates them or leaves them flat. When it's going well, they're happy. When it's not, they grow discontented and leave. A young associate at Goldman Sachs, who joined the firm after spending a year with another prestigious investment bank, was eloquent about the difference between the two firms. At Goldman, he told us, the managing directors responded positively—and quickly—when he sought more work and new challenges, whereas similar requests (from him and other young colleagues) at the previous firm never merited a response. Firms that excel in developing young stars understand this dynamic and make it work for them and their young stars. As Rajat Gupta, the managing partner of McKinsey, explains, "Far and away the most important dimension of development is on the job. . . . Dealing with real-life situations is where the majority of a consultant's learning occurs."

This explains why deployment is such a crucial piece of the equation in developing young stars. Nothing matters more than putting the right person in the right assignment. And since it's unlikely that this will just "happen," it means building the firm's capacity to match its professionals' individual needs and skills with client opportunities.

At American Management Systems, where business units operate autonomously to a large degree and where the rapid growth in the number of employees during the past two decades has complicated the task of keeping track of them, that means having a central human resource information system. It also means having about thirty-five people who trained in employee relations on hand to act as consultants to the various business units in staffing matters. And, it means having an individual staffing system in place for each individual business unit, so that the firm knows who is coming on board, or who is coming free from what assignment, what their skills are, and what projects are coming down the pipeline that might suit them.

At Latham & Watkins, it means having an option for recruits in their first two years at the firm to be placed in the "Unassigned System," which is run by the firm's Associates Committee. New recruits who choose to be in this system, and they are encouraged to do so, gain experience in a wide variety of areas, rather than immediately being assigned to one practice area. How does this system work? When a partner has a particular matter he needs an associate to work on, he brings it to the Associates Committee along with an estimate of the time needed to complete the work. The committee then matches the project with an associate who is available and who has an interest in that type of work. The committee tries to give each associate a balanced—and manageable—assortment of work, and also takes care to match associates with a variety of different partners. Managing partner Bob Dell explained:

> Fighting the battle against specialization is important in our firm. Young associates are so focused, sometimes. You know, "I want to be a litigator. I don't want to do corporate." We try to give them a higher concentration of the kind of work they want, but we also want them to experience other things.
>
> We also try to move people around so that they work with a variety of other people because you experience different styles and learn different things from different people. The process is also a great way to allocate resources, by the way. If you stick someone on a team, and that team isn't particularly busy for a given month, that person simply isn't busy. This way, while you're exposing people to different types of work, you're also moving resources where the work is.[1]

Focusing on on-the-job learning doesn't preclude off-site seminars and formal educational programs. All these firms offer formal programs of some type, generally designed to introduce a particular skill or topic to a large group of people or to bring everyone up to speed on a particular issue at the same time. In some instances, these programs are necessary and a piece of what motivates associates to explore new areas or to excel at a particular discipline. But even in firms where formal study is considered very important, it takes a backseat to the day-to-day work of the firm.

Real-time feedback is the second crucial piece of on-the-job experience for young stars. Older partners at Goldman Sachs often joke about getting their first "performance reviews" in the men's room, from the former senior partner and renowned trader Gus Levy. This is the kind of developmental feedback we're talking about here: not the once- or twice-a-year formal review process, but the "hey, you did a good job with that presentation today, and here are a couple of things you might try next time" kind.

Real-time feedback is far more effective in helping young people learn than eleven-months-after-the-fact postmortems of projects they can barely remember. This informal, immediate feedback is also tremendously motivating. When a senior professional takes the time to explain why a project is being handled the way it is or challenges a young associate to think beyond her specific task, he's not only strengthening her technical skills but also demonstrating the firm's concern for her development. Through these conversations, which take place in the halls, or over meals, or on plane rides back to the office, young stars have the opportunity to develop relationships with more experienced leaders. Often, they will blossom into true mentoring relationships as well, providing young stars with role models and guides.

Making the Grade

People who join PSFs are accustomed to competition and to being successful. They don't like getting Bs, let alone Cs. And a lot of them don't even like A minuses. It doesn't matter if it's a class, athletic event, or client assignment. When they perform, they want to know how they've done, and if they've gotten a B or a C they want to know why. So if you want to motivate them, and you want the quality of their work to improve, you can't give out all As, and you have to tell them, thoughtfully and candidly, why you rated their performance as you did.

Effective performance feedback systems—the formal kind—are also an essential tool in developing stars. In all the firms we studied, annual, or even biannual, performance reviews are a fact of life for professional staff: in their first year, in their second year, and, as we'll see in chapter 5, in their twentieth year. Typically, project leaders are asked to evaluate every member of their team, on every assignment.

These data are then compiled electronically so that they can be sent to the appropriate reviewers when the formal process begins. The care the Associates Committee at Latham & Watkins devotes to conducting full and fair reviews is representative. All that time and thoughtfulness are wasted, however, if the partners responsible for each associate don't then have forthright conversations with them.

Regularly scheduled performance reviews are useful in helping associates understand where they need to grow or improve, and what they need to focus on learning. Because they give people the information they need to put their own performance in context, they can be useful in other ways as well. For one, it clarifies why they are being compensated as they are.

Although recruits usually start off in lockstep, with compensation packages based on their credentials and entry level, in many firms they begin to diverge pretty quickly thereafter. If you are giving some people As, and other people Cs, you've got to pay the people who are getting As more. How much more is for you to decide, based on how your organization is structured, how you handle partner compensation, and so forth. But you must make the difference between an A performance and a C performance tangible. Candid performance discussions help people understand why they are where they are relative to their peers.

Candor can also help people decide for themselves whether the firm is right for them and vice versa. As one senior leader observed, "We don't have a formal 'up or out' policy. We don't say 'if you're not a manager in three years, you're gone.' But we do give direct feedback, and the consequence is that if we tell somebody multiple times over a two-year period that they're not doing well, they usually decide to leave. The people we hire are impatient. They don't want to be last in their class."

Giving people honest feedback about their performance and the room to decide the implications for themselves doesn't always work. Often you do have to help people realize it's time to move on, and we'll turn to that next. But at a minimum, formal reviews can be a useful goad for partners who'd rather not be the bearers of bad news. As Alan Sheldon, vice chairman and managing director at Young &

Rubicam, explained, "If they're not going to make it here, they will need to make it somewhere else. [Letting them know that] is the fair thing to do. Just not the easy thing."

Alumni, Not Dropouts

Identifying, attracting, and retaining stars is a continuum, and individuals evolve at different rates along it. The process is similar to a marathon. At the beginning of the race, everybody is together at the starting line. One hundred yards out, they're still together, and even at a mile, most will still be neck and neck. But come mile twenty, they're not together anymore. Many will have fallen behind; and a few will be pushing even farther into the lead. The same phenomenon exists in organizations. Some people may start out fast and then slow down. Others may start slow and accelerate later on. The speed with which people develop in their careers differs markedly from person to person, a truth you can never forget as you nurture young talent.

Nevertheless, there does come a point when you know that someone isn't going to make it in your firm. This doesn't mean that he or she isn't a great person. It just means that the fit isn't there. What do you do with this knowledge? How do you deal with the people you believe won't make it over the long term?

Many firms ignore the problem in the hope that it will somehow take care of itself. If you choose this route, you have to expect that some B or C players will linger indefinitely, delivering client work that's below par and infecting the place with mediocrity. Most, however, will leave on their own, sooner or later, because they aren't getting promoted. And when they leave, do you think they will feel well treated? Probably not. Will they identify potential clients for you when they bump into opportunities out in the marketplace? Probably not, because they'll think you didn't give them a fair chance.

There are two real art forms in managing this continuum of developing stars. One is making certain that your system is aligned around the top performers—those professionals who are going to be tomorrow's stars and drive the success of your firm. The other is making sure that those who don't fit depart in a way that generates benefits, for them and for the firm, without incurring huge costs.

Many PSFs facilitate outplacement by practicing a policy of lifetime affiliation. This policy is premised on the idea that all of the firm's employees are members of the same great team. Some of them will stay at the firm and do great things, while others will leave and do great things. But all of them, without exception, will do great things. In fact, most of the firms in our study carry this thinking so far that they refer to their former employees as alumni.

Pause for a moment on that word, *alumni*. Think about how alumni relate to their alma mater. Alumni are people whose help and participation are crucial to the success of their schools, even though they are no longer present on campus. Schools organize alumni conferences, publish alumni bulletins, and build alumni Web sites because alumni are such an important source of funds.

Professional firm alumni, too, can be an important source of revenue for a firm. One consulting firm we know receives almost a third of its new business from its alumni. In addition to adding revenue, alumni are critical in defining a firm's strategic identity (as discussed in chapter 3). They are a highly credible "inside" source of information about the firm's capabilities. Alumni from your firm may be talking about you this minute—to possible future clients and to possible future recruits. Are they saying, "Yeah, you ought to call my old firm. They're the best in the world"? Or are they saying, "Yeah, I used to work there; they're terrible"? Or are they simply holding their tongues? You'll never hear the kudos you're being given out in the marketplace, just as you'll never hear the critiques voiced when you're not around. But they exist, and their influence grows by the day.

In most PSFs, turnover rates run between 10 and 20 percent per year. That means it doesn't take long before a firm has far more alumni than employees. And who has more credibility with potential clients? People who are at the firm peddling something, or people who used to be at the firm who aren't peddling anything and no longer have a vested interest in its success? As Earle Yaffa, managing director at

Skadden Arps, said, "We are happy to have [alumni] in positions like assistant counsel or general counsel, where we can continue to work with them. It's absolutely a good source of business."

Jack Walker, former managing partner at Latham & Watkins, says that at his firm, "up until about ten years ago, it was a negative experience all around if somebody left—even if we were ambivalent about it. But now, when someone leaves, we're still sad, humanly, but we try to help that person be placed. We're very active with place-ment, in fact. And that has turned out to be such an engine of business for us. Not only at the associate level, but also at the partner level."

For these reasons, outstanding firms help people leave a firm well—as Walker says, "with dignity, and also with time." As Walker also notes, building a network of alumni is "a sign of maturing in an or-ganization like this." It takes an environment in which there is a strong sense of sustainability—of durability—to realize that when people leave, "it's not necessarily a failure, it's an opportunity."

At the end of the day, the people who create that environment—a context in which everyone grows, the people who leave as well as the people who stay—are a firm's senior stars. In a word, the young stars we've talked about here, "all grown up."

In the next chapter we'll look at how great firms guide and moti-vate their senior stars.

5 ★ Guiding Your Brightest Stars

The Three-Hat Challenge

I F THE people you pay are more important over time than the people who pay you, the people you pay the most—your most experienced stars—are the most important of all. Who are these accomplished stars? From information technology consultants to accounting firms, they go by a variety of titles: executive vice president, managing director, vice president, partner. But in all cases, they are the organization's leaders, the men and women who are responsible for initiating and managing client relationships and projects, for building offices and practices, for training and mentoring the young talent who will become the leaders of tomorrow.

Partner-level stars are a professional service firm's scarcest and most valuable resource. Whether the firm succeeds or fails depends on their performance and leadership: How wisely and productively they allocate their time. How effectively they fulfill their client and management responsibilities. How committed they are to the long-term prosperity and growth of the firm. Success depends, in short, on the degree to which the firm's goals are these stars' goals—and vice versa.

Alignment between the firm's goals and the individual goals of its stars isn't automatic, however. Ultimately, both the firm's people systems and its structure and governance are critical elements in bringing it about. (See figure 5-1.) One reason the challenge is so great is the set of tensions that are inherent in the star's position, the competing needs and priorities that come from simultaneously being a *producer,* a *manager,* and an *owner.* We call this the *three-hat challenge.*

Professionals rarely become partners or move into senior management positions unless they are excellent producers. Client work is challenging and rewarding, personally and financially, and they're great at it. So, however much senior stars may enjoy the recognition that comes with promotion, they don't want to stop producing professional work. Nor does the firm expect them to. On the contrary,

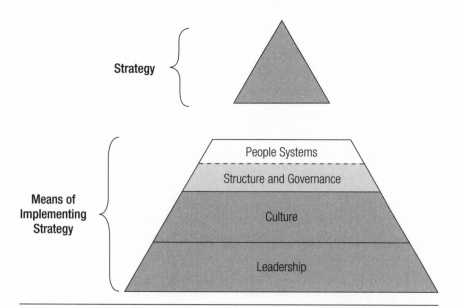

Figure 5-1   **Alignment Pyramid: Guiding Accomplished Stars**

bringing in and serving new clients is the primary source of recognition in PSFs as well as their economic lifeblood.

At the same time, promotion carries with it growing responsibility for the management, leadership, and governance of the firm. Every senior professional is expected to take on routine day-to-day management responsibilities (such as feedback, coaching, and performance reviews) for the people she supervises. Over time, some will be asked to add formal management positions as office heads, practice leaders, or committee chairs to their agendas as well. In addition, all of the senior stars expect—and are expected—to participate in key decisions that accompany their status as owners of the firm, such as partner promotions, selection of the senior leader, and new strategic initiatives.

In principle this sounds straightforward. In practice it is immensely challenging because the demands and horizons of a senior star's three roles are distinctly different. As producers, stars are wholly focused on serving and selling clients *now*. As managers, they have to devote time and attention to the people assigned to them and the organizational units for which they're responsible. They are responsible for and care about the long-term destiny of the firm, which means investing both time and money to build its future prosperity and health.

For the individual who must serve clients and fulfill firm responsibilities simultaneously, the pressing question is always "How do I spend my time?" This is the critical tension professionals experience as producer–managers. As a producer–owner, the question is "How do I balance my needs today against the needs of future partner generations?" And as a manager–owner, the question is "How do I balance the needs of my office or practice area against the needs of the firm?" (Conflicts between individual stars or among groups in the firm are rooted in similar questions. Can you think of a PSF in which the rainmakers and managers never disagree about how to apportion the firm's profits? Or a firm that hasn't struggled at least once with competing claims from the senior—often semiretired—partners who built it and the younger partners now doing the heavy lifting?)

The pressure points for three-hat challenges are money and time. In PSFs these amount to the same thing, so it can be tempting to think of them purely as resource allocation problems that can be solved (if not eliminated) by the right people systems. Tempting, but wrong.

Consider compensation. A good compensation system can mitigate three-hat tensions, but it cannot make them go away. Money that's used to reward a partner for developing associates can't be used to reward another partner for client work. Funds invested in opening new offices won't be available for the current year's compensation pool. The decisions individual partners and firms must make to resolve three-hat challenges require real tradeoffs. That's why they're so difficult, and why even the mechanisms available to reduce the pressure can only go so far.

Further complicating the situation is the nature of professionals themselves. When stars become partners, they take on new roles and responsibilities, not new personalities. In many respects, they're simply grown-up versions of their intelligent, competitive, independent, and insecure younger selves. Not surprisingly, therefore, promotion heightens (but doesn't change) their fundamental need to seek fresh challenges or their equally strong distaste for being told what to do. Autonomy is a key component of the value proposition for all professionals, and this is particularly true at the partner level, where the desire for independence tends to grow exponentially with career and client successes.

Not so long ago, many firms could sidestep the issue of autonomy by simply allowing their senior stars to pursue their own interests. In the more forgiving competitive environment that used to characterize the sector, this approach wasn't all bad. When times are flush (as during the last decade), firms tend to run greater risks by overmanaging star professionals than they do by undermanaging them.

In times of economic turmoil, however, when new competitors appear and disappear in the same week and demand for your services fluctuates every month as it has during the first years of the twenty-first century, a laissez-faire approach becomes a recipe for disaster. Why? Because firms can no longer avoid developing "real" coherent competitive strategies. Their survival will depend in large part on their stars' *ability* and *willingness* to align themselves with the firm's goals.

The result is a paradox, which is *the* central management challenge facing professional firms: On the one hand, firms have to manage their partners. Retaining, motivating, and effectively deploying these valuable assets is the key to financial and competitive success. On the other hand, the idea of "managing" partners is an oxymoron. An old joke says it all: Managing established and experienced lawyers (or creative directors or consultants) is like herding cats.

Guiding Not Managing

What gives the joke its bite is the fact that professionals are among the world's most independent people. Tell them to go "here" and they may go "there" just because. But the metaphor, while cute, has a fatal flaw: It misrepresents both the distribution of power and the nature of leadership in a PSF. For one, it is the so-called cats that have the power—the firm's formal leader serves to a large extent at their pleasure. Equally important, leadership in PSFs is personal as well as positional.

Although certain positions, such as managing partner and office manager, carry formal leadership responsibilities, any and all of a firm's senior people have the potential to exercise leadership every day. The reason is that the central test of leadership is the ability to influence others to do things that they might not do if left to their own devices.

In PSFs such influence is derived almost wholly from personal behavior: partners respond to other partners, more because of their trust and confidence in them than because they occupy specific roles. Individuals exercise leadership less by virtue of formal authority than because other powerful partners willingly *follow* them. Leadership in PSFs is less about grandiose visions or rousing speeches than it is about motivating others to behave in the best interests of the firm. People accept client assignments, transfer offices, and shift between "producer" and "manager" responsibilities in part because someone exerted personal leadership, and they followed.

This reality is why the partner-level stars with the most impact lead from within the partnership, rather than from above it, even if they hold formal leadership positions. Would you willingly follow someone whom you perceived to be arrogant? Or self-centered? Or controlling? Of course not! Effective leaders respect and trust other people. They are deeply grounded in their firm's values and beliefs, and they are genuinely oriented toward helping other professionals succeed. Partners and younger colleagues follow these men and women because they believe they want to help them achieve their full potential and the firm achieve its goals. For the aggressive and competitive stars who typically populate PSFs, this form of leadership may seem counterintuitive. Professionals succeed on the basis of their personal skills and accomplishments: Selling and serving clients is the overarching competency. Individual client achievements are highly visible and vigorously celebrated. Leadership from within is less visible and easily ignored, especially since the most effective leaders rarely draw attention to their achievements. Nevertheless, this kind of personal leadership is essential to guide a firm's stars in the direction of its goals. It is also the invisible fuel that propels a firm's people systems.

If a firm's formal systems for managing its professionals constitute the hardware, then leadership is the software that drives those systems. It determines the efficacy of the firm's promotion and compensation decisions and the consequences of its performance management systems. Without leadership, review processes will not influence stars' behavior, nor will stars be effectively deployed. Any firm can design elegant procedures or imitate the practices of rival firms. How those procedures are implemented is what differentiates outstanding firms and eventually contributes to their competitive advantage.

You Are Whom You Promote

We've said that professional firms are the people they hire. Nowhere are the consequences of this fact as stark as they are in partner-level promotions (by which we mean promotion to any position that carries with it a significant ownership stake and leadership responsibility). Why? The strength of the partnership determines the future value of the firm, period. The partners define the capabilities of the firm. They drive the economics of the firm. In the aggregate, they define the internal and external strategic identity of the firm.

Poor promotion decisions are expensive any way you reckon them. Partners who don't epitomize the firm's values and culture, or whose performance is below par, undermine its credibility with clients and with the rest of the staff. Retaining them always draws down the firm's economic value. The only question is "How fast?" At the same time, phasing out your mistakes after they've been partners for a short time, two years say, is costly in a different way. It sends younger stars the message that "promotion here is risky," and may encourage the most talented to leave before they are even considered for partnership. This is why great firms (and firms that would be great) are as careful about the promotion process itself as they are about evaluating the capabilities of the candidates.

Process Matters

The best PSFs look at promotion decisions from the perspective of the firm's future as well as the candidate's past. In firms that practice "rear-view decision making," promotion is basically a reward for the work a candidate has already done. In forward-looking firms, promotion reflects not only the candidate's record to date but also the partners' confidence that she will continue to be an extraordinarily valuable colleague over the course of her career.

Gus Blackshear, managing partner at Fulbright & Jaworski, discussed promotion: "First of all, of course, we want people who do excellent legal work. And then you look at the other items. How are they going to do at training people? What kind of colleague are they going to be? Can they help you develop your practice?"

Promotion criteria have to weigh past performance heavily because that is the only fact base the firm has to work from. But promotion decisions should also be tempered by judgments about the candidate's long-term potential, even though there will be plenty of pressure *not* to look too far ahead. Think how compelling the arguments can be to promote a high-powered producer whose values are somewhat inconsistent with the firm's. Or all the reasons that people will adduce to bring on a likable young associate with adequate skills whose commitment has been steadfast. He has clearly given his all. His promotion will demonstrate that the firm is vibrant and growing. A "yes" decision will make everyone feel good.

Good promotion processes help to offset such pressures. While the specifics vary from firm to firm (and profession to profession), good processes share several characteristics. First, the organization has explicit criteria and standards. Its senior people know what they are looking for, not just in terms of capabilities and skills but also in terms of attitudes and values. Second, the process itself is rigorous and driven by data. Third, partnership decisions are firmwide decisions, not office or individual decisions. Broad consensus building is an essential part of the process; everyone has to buy in, directly or through representatives they trust.

Together, these three characteristics go a long way toward depoliticizing the promotion process. The objective is to create a process based on capability rather than advocacy. For this reason, many firms also separate recommending authority from decision authority. They vest the latter in institutions such as promotion committees or the full partnership, whose sole responsibility is to think about the long-term value of each candidate to the firm as a whole as opposed to one practice or single geography.

What we have just described is embodied in the partner promotion process at Latham & Watkins. According to Larry Stein, chairman of the firm's Associates Committee, there is a four-prong partnership standard: teamwork, commitment, first-chair lawyering ability, and potential for business development.

The promotion process is essentially a continuation of the rigorous review process described in chapter 4. In an associate's sixth year, her major supervisors are given confidential "on deck" questionnaires to complete, with an eye toward giving the associate a sense of whether or not she is on track to become a partner. Among the questions: What was this associate's high-water mark? What is their business development potential? How does this person compare to people whom we have recently admitted to the partnership or recently decided not to admit to the partnership? In the seventh year, the supervisors fill out a confidential "partnership questionnaire," designed to home in even closer on the individual's progress and potential to make partner. "When someone is up for partner," Stein noted, "we actually fan out and interview all of their supervisors, one on one."

Building consensus is thus very much part of the process. The partnership vote at Latham & Watkins is held in November, and during the summer, Stein said,

> We spend a great deal of time making sure we all agree that [any given candidate] is on track for partnership or not on track. That's when the big debates get held.
>
> I think all of the time and work is worth it. People have a real respect for the process. We're not infallible, but we listen to everyone, we do our best, and the partners all feel like they have super-adequate opportunities to put their two cents in along the line. By the time we reach November, people have all gotten behind it [and] the voting goes pretty smoothly.
>
> It requires an 85 percent vote of the partnership to admit a partner here. That's a high standard.

Korn/Ferry uses criteria and a peer review method similar to Latham & Watkins's to evaluate professionals up for partnership. Their criteria include relationships with clients, relationships within the firm, business development, and execution on assignments. A committee composed of a group of partners conducts the evaluations. Members go out and conduct 360-degree reviews, talking with everyone the individuals in question have worked with or for inside the firm. (While the process does not involve talking with clients, the firm does have an extensive client feedback system.) Then the committee makes its recommendation to the firm's leaders, who make the ultimate decision.

Alternative Paths to Retaining Experienced Stars

Traditionally, the path to partnership or comparable senior status was straightforward. Young professionals spent the first few years developing their professional skills. Those who made it over that hurdle would spend the next few years working more independently and learning to manage client projects and to develop business. Then, somewhere between six and ten years out, depending on the industry, the survivors would be considered for admission to the partnership. Those who didn't make it left (often helped by the firm to find a soft landing). Those who did make it could be partners for life.

Today, both the up-or-out model, which requires professionals to leave if they are not "partner material," and the assurance that partnership is forever are giving way. The reasons for this are related to the changing needs and desires of both professionals and organizations. For stars, leaving a partnership to seek new challenges has become far more common than it was twenty or thirty years ago. Some have aspirations to start their own company, while others want to spend more time with their families. Some even want to stay in the firm without the added load of becoming a partner: They want to practice their profession but don't care to have a significant ownership stake or management responsibility in the firm.

For the organizations, the challenges are twofold. They need increasing numbers of experienced people with specialized skills outside their own areas of expertise. They are also finding that they want to hold on (at reasonable cost) to professionals who are great contributors but, for one reason or another, aren't partner material.

At Fulbright & Jaworski, for example, lawyers who do not become partners may become "of-counsel" attorneys. According to partner Steve Pfeiffer, the of-counsel position allows the firm to retain the benefits of someone with outstanding skills in a certain legal area who may not have the skills to attract and manage or expand client relationships. "An of-counsel position in a law firm can allow a particular attorney to excel in areas of the law which he or she knows best rather than requiring such a person to perform in a more traditional 'partner' role which may not suit his or her aspirations or circumstances."

Latham & Watkins, too, has of-counsel positions as well as two categories of partnership: equity partner and income partner.

"The main difference between equity partner and income partner," one partner explained, "is that the equity partner function assumes a high degree of capability in a lot of areas, not just good lawyering. You are expected to develop business, to manage large client relationships, and to have a level of commitment that allows you to do all that and maintain a very full practice load at the same time. I don't think there is one single model for the income-partner designation, but it's generally somebody who's a fine lawyer in his or her field but doesn't hit all the other bells. To the outside world there is not much distinction."

Internally, he noted, many people who hold of-counsel and income partner positions "are happy to have that title." For a whole host of reasons such as family commitments or life-balance issues, he said, "they don't want to take on the added expectations that go with moving to a different status."

At Goldman Sachs, before its IPO, individuals who weren't voted into the partnership often became "extended managing directors" (EMDs) and served as nonpartner leaders in the firm. And, as former chairman and CEO Jon Corzine was quick to point out, the EMD slot did not mean that partnership was forever out of the question. "It's a mezzanine position," he told us. "It's one that has value economically and status-wise, but it's not the same as partner. Over time, a third of [our EMDs] at any given point will probably make it to partner. And there will also be people who will spend their whole career as a managing director without becoming partner."

Before the alternative position was established at Goldman Sachs, Corzine said, the gap between the partners and the rest of the firm was too great. "It was too black and white," he said. "And I think it was hurting our ability to develop the managerial class in the organization. So it's worth the risk. What we've done is push the so-called up-or-out threshold lower into the firm's performance management system. People say 'If I can't even be one of those guys, what am I doing here?' The result is we see turnover in the group that doesn't quite make EMD. People that are ten years in and haven't made it really feel an up-or-out push."

Amid all these changes is the challenging question of lateral hires. Bringing in a partner-level professional is complicated on two dimensions. One is the signal it can send to younger people in the firm, who often perceive (rightly or not) that it diminishes their own opportunities because there are only so many senior slots. The other is the obvious difficulty of assessing how the lateral hire will affect the firm's gene pool. When you make a lateral hire, you have to weigh the advantages—experienced talent and established client relationships—and possible disadvantages—bad habits learned at the earlier firm, which can quickly infiltrate your firm and poison the culture or de-motivate employees who feel overlooked in favor of outsiders. If your new lateral hire is a gifted creature who brings with him several key accounts, but quickly alienates the team of younger professionals he is meant to lead, your firm is worse off for the hire in the long run.

Compensation: No Single Answer

At Wachtell, Lipton, the partners' annual compensation goes up in lockstep for fifteen years. After that, the compensation remains the same year after year, and each partner makes the same amount as every other partner who has been at the firm for fifteen or more years. At Bain, partner compensation is based on individual, office, and firm performance. At Heidrick & Struggles, there is an established range of compensation for partners, but each partner is paid within the range according to individual performance. At Ernst & Young, each partner is required to keep 50 percent of his earnings as capital in the firm each year. That means if a partner has higher earnings one year than he did the prior year, he has to pay 50 percent of the difference into the firm. If his earnings are lower, he takes out 50 percent of the difference.

While these practices differ sharply, each is effective for the same reason—it doesn't get in the way. Each system allows the firm to distribute financial rewards in ways that support its goals and reinforce its values. It's also perceived to be fair by members of the firm: Partners think that they are compensated appropriately for their own efforts and vis-à-vis their colleagues.

Compensation questions don't have right (or wrong) answers. A policy that is perfect for one organization can be a disaster for another. The acid test is *alignment:* whether the performance the compensation system's incentives encourage is the performance the firm wants to reward. If a firm's strategy calls for international expansion, for example, but its compensation system doesn't reward senior stars for picking up stakes and moving, new, international offices are unlikely to flourish. Similarly, if the firm says it values nurturing and developing young stars, but rewards senior people exclusively for billable hours, everyone—especially its young talent—will be acutely aware of the discrepancy. Whatever else gaps like these between the firm's rhetoric and the reality of its cash flows may foster, it certainly is not management's credibility.

To complicate matters further, even the "right" set of answers won't remain right forever. The dynamics of competition and the firm's evolving goals inevitably generate new demands and strategic priorities. It's common for firms to make ad hoc adjustments to their compensation systems to accommodate these needs. But precisely because these are systems, one-off changes can drive them out of alignment as well as send conflicting signals about what the firm truly values.

Although there aren't any universal best practices for compensation systems, there are a few common denominators among the ones that are most effective. First, everyone trusts the decision-making process—and the decision makers—to be fair. One mechanism often used to build trust and reinforce fairness is transparency. At many law firms, for example, every partner knows what every other partner is making. Other firms, such as Goldman Sachs, create firmwide committees that meet annually to review and sometimes change compensation guidelines and to ensure that the various divisions haven't gotten out of sync with one another in terms of compensation.

Whatever the method, trust is crucial. As David McAuliffe, COO and managing director at Hambrecht & Quist, told us, "Fairness is the most important thing you could ever have in an organization, because if people feel like [the compensation process] is fair, and they understand what the rules are, then they'll feel like their contributions are being recognized."

A second common denominator is that the system is designed to encourage partners to take the long view and to focus on the firm's strategic goals. This is what partnership, having an ownership stake in the firm, has done for decades, and what equity ownership in public professional firms is designed to accomplish today. The best firms, however, have appreciated the importance of equity-like participation since well before professional organizations had any need to think about going public to increase their access to capital.

At McKinsey (which remains a private corporation), for example, partners have always received equity ownership in the firm as part of their compensation. Over time they accumulate this ownership, but the stock they hold cannot be sold to anyone outside the firm. When they retire or die, it must be sold back to the firm. Not only is this an important piece of senior compensation that makes people feel like partners in the firm but it is also a way to transfer ownership in the firm from generation to generation.

At Grey Advertising, giving partners equity in the firm has long been part of the compensation system. (The percentage of the firm actually owned by the public is small.) In the United States, for example, the partner compensation package has had two elements for the last twenty years: first, a base salary and a year-end cash bonus, and second, a "senior management incentive plan" offered to the forty or so top people at the firm. The plan allocates some money that is put in escrow, to come out at the end of every five-year period. It also puts some money toward Grey shares. As Ed Meyer, chairman, CEO, and president, explains, "It's a modest golden handcuff, and it also provides some financial discipline for people who might need it. If you got a hundred thousand dollars, for example, we might allocate fifty thousand to cash in your escrow account and fifty in effect to phantom shares, which will ultimately be real Grey shares. At the end of the period, you get both cash and stock in the typical plan. And the stock historically will have appreciated significantly so that half of your allocation will have doubled, and the other half will have earned interest."

Third, outstanding firms are explicit and inventive about the measures they use to evaluate performance and determine partner compensation. On this topic, PSFs are no different from any other organization: You get what you pay for, and what you pay for is rooted in what you measure. The problem is that it's easy to measure revenue, billable hours, and other "hard" indices of short-term financial performance. But it's hard to capture the subtler aspects of partners' contributions (such as mentoring young people or idea development), and it's virtually impossible to measure the long-term present value of each partner's work. A client who paid huge sums of money may turn out to be a liability that could severely damage external strategic identity, for example, because she thinks the firm's work is lousy and lets the world know that. By the same token, the word of mouth from an ecstatic smaller client may create the greatest advertising "campaign" the firm has ever had.

Firms that are serious about developing the next generation and building client assets (in addition to client revenues) devise ways to get around this fundamental disconnect between easily measured, economic contributions per partner and actual *value* per partner. Some, for example, conduct anonymous exit interviews with departing talent in addition to collecting feedback from the young stars partners are supervising. Some measure client retention and solicit feedback from former clients as well as those who are now paying the bills. All this is used to judge a partner's effectiveness. To get a full picture of each partner's contributions to the firm's well-being, they also carry out extensive peer reviews.

All of these "soft" measures have limitations beyond the fact that they can't be quantified the way that financial measures can. Each involves some degree of subjectivity. Each depends on people's willingness to engage in candid, and often difficult, discussions. The saving grace is that a little goes a long way. The very fact that the firm solicits upward feedback or looks at what happens to clients after the firm has completed its work creates behavioral change. The measures don't have to be perfect. They do have to line up with the goals and values the firm has set out to pursue and ease the most predictable tensions these goals and values will create.

Performance Management: Units of One

How many times have you been surprised by the retirement of a partner-level colleague or the sudden departure of a superstar producer? Were the reasons they gave you even more surprising? You've worked with someone for ten or twenty years and suddenly you realize that he is reevaluating the priorities and values that have driven you both since the beginning of your careers. Perhaps his ideas made you think about your own future. For most of your adult life you've committed every ounce of energy to this organization, and now all the upward incentives seem to be gone. Suddenly, the firm and the values you've helped reinforce don't look like such a clear priority. What will it be that makes you stay?

The answer to this question is one of the most important points of action for the leadership group of a professional firm. If it's "Because you're one of us" or, worse, if no one even notices the question is being asked, the game is over. Loyalty is a virtue, but it's not compelling in the abstract. It's reasonable, as well as predictable, for a partner who is spending 90 percent of her time with clients to be thinking more about what's happening outside the firm (and inside her own head) than about the needs of the firm. To retain and motivate this partner, the firm has to respond appropriately to her professional and personal needs. And it must be able to do the same thing for each of her peers, who find themselves in different circumstances with different needs. This is difficult under any conditions, but it is particularly hard when a firm and its stars have gotten out of touch.

Professional service firms tend to have a pretty good grasp of their junior stars' skills and aspirations because their senior stars are directly involved in their development. But this involvement often falls off sharply (if it doesn't disappear altogether) once the stars have been promoted to partner-level. There are all sorts of plausible reasons for the change. The stars have proved they can perform; that's why they've been given their new positions. There's always a new crop of youngsters who need time and attention. Besides, the last thing experienced professionals want is to be told what to do.

Nevertheless, the same needs and expectations are still there: to achieve financial independence, to keep on learning and growing, to satisfy their personal goals as well as their professional ambitions, and to feel that their views and voices matter and that their contributions are appreciated. Addressing these needs is intrinsically challenging and becomes more so with time. Why? The dynamics of three-hat conflicts are one complication. The facts of life are another. People's priorities change (and diverge) as their careers and personal lives evolve. At one stage, sixty- or seventy-hour weeks are exhilaratingly intense; later, they're just intensely exhausting. Sometimes money matters more than recognition; other times the opposite is true. The only thing a firm can be sure of is that its partners are bound to see and value things differently when they are newly admitted than they will when they're having a midlife crisis or nearing retirement.

At firms in which the partners' contributions continue to deepen, organization and culture are important parts of the story, as we'll see in later chapters. But retaining and motivating senior stars also requires a robust performance management process, which includes formal elements, such as compensation and performance reviews, as well as informal feedback, coaching, and mentoring. Partner-level compensation reviews are standard operating procedure in many (maybe most) PSFs. Regular performance reviews, for everyone in the organization from the CEO on down, are not. In our view they should be.

The Power of Partner Performance Reviews

To say that it's hard to give colleagues feedback is an understatement. When the colleagues are also your partners and the firm's co-owners, it can look downright impossible. Performance reviews are time intensive. They're awkward. There are a hundred and one reasons to avoid them. The problem is that without them, neither the stars nor the firm are apt to realize their full potential. That is why most of the outstanding firms we've studied require every senior professional to engage regularly in a formal performance review and objective-setting process.

Establishing firmwide strategic goals and setting standards of behavior is one thing. Hard-wiring them into an organization is another. As we've noted before, the only way to steer a PSF is to guide the stars who make it up—professionals who are guided first and foremost by their own goals and beliefs. Realistically, the most effective leverage any firm has to motivate and shape its stars' behavior comes from its capacity to influence the goals they set for themselves and the values they internalize.

Because performance reviews are a vehicle for setting goals and articulating performance standards, they provide an opportunity for the firm to influence its stars and vice versa. Whether this actually happens hinges a great deal on how the review process is conceived and managed. When reviews are a cover for bureaucracy—or worse, playing "got'cha"—trust disappears. Without trust, influence evaporates. In healthy systems, reviews are a mechanism for an ongoing dialogue designed to help the firm know its stars and the stars know themselves. Where this is the case, the possibilities for trust and influence are real and substantial.

At Bain, all partners, even those at the most senior level, receive rigorous annual performance reviews on multiple dimensions: client contributions, people development, knowledge contribution, reputation building, and "one-firm" behavior. A committee of appointed partners is charged with the task of evaluating each individual partner in concert with office heads and the chief executive. The process is both data driven and judgmental, requiring hundreds of person-hours each year. It culminates in personalized feedback surrounding a partner's performance, compensation, career plan, and HLAs (highly leveraged accomplishments, or future goals). No one is exempt: A special subcommittee interviews partners and assesses the chief executive's performance against previous objectives, providing him with a lengthy written report card that ultimately influences his compensation.

"We set increasingly high standards for partner performance," explains John Donahoe, Bain's current chief executive. "Performance goes well beyond the short-term financial contribution. It emphasizes a partner's value added toward building multiyear assets—client assets, people assets, knowledge assets. Does he or she truly contribute toward building an outstanding firm and generating genuine client success stories? We collect mountains of data ranging from upward feedback to peer reviews to client performance. Partners complete lengthy self-assessments centered around the results they helped their clients achieve. Overall, the review process strongly reinforces our values, while increasing quality and performance standards."

Like promotion decisions, good performance reviews begin by looking backward, at what's been accomplished since the last review. But even when a senior star is underperforming, the balance of a good discussion will tip toward the future—to what can be accomplished and what ought to be done. In fact, the potential to motivate tomorrow's behavior is a primary reason to include formal reviews in a firm's performance management system. Particularly for stars who have just been promoted, reviews are a powerful forum in which to convey the message "you're not there yet, there's always room to grow" and to begin to set expectations about how their roles in the firm will evolve over time. Conversely, when someone isn't performing, reviews provide a forcing mechanism for the firm and the star to look at what's happening and to develop plans for a new assignment or perhaps even eventual outplacement that will preserve the star's dignity and the firm's quality.

The chief challenge in performance reviews is developing a full and fair picture of each individual's contributions. As with compensation, systems that collect only "hard" data can easily miss important aspects of the longer-term value someone is creating for the firm. "Soft" data are significant.

Goldman Sachs looks at qualitative criteria such as judgment, ability to develop relations with clients, and technical skills, along with mentoring, coaching, recruiting, and leadership. McKinsey's partner reviews evaluate client impact and firm impact rather than how much the partner is producing. At Grey Advertising, evaluations cover whether professionals are "hopeful, inspirational, and helpful to their colleagues," whether they are energetic, and whether they demonstrate "over-and-above-what's-demanded performance, day in and day out."

How do you actually evaluate whether someone is "inspirational" or "hopeful"? Truly exploring these qualities requires careful observation, deep reflection, and excellent communication. It requires asking the right question and coming back and asking it differently if it doesn't work the first time. It requires a commitment to establishing the "facts" of each partner's performance, as he and his colleagues see them. A tough task, and a big commitment of time and emotional energy. Outstanding firms are willing to make that commitment.

Building on Strength

Fully developed performance reviews require a lot of time, both from the person who's being reviewed and from the reviewers. The return on this investment is knowledge and insight that can be used to take the value created through performance evaluation to the next level—customizing senior stars' roles and responsibilities throughout their careers. Why customize? The whole point of a performance management system is to help stars manage their careers so that they create the greatest possible value for the firm and for themselves. The way that happens is to help them build on strength.

Every individual has a set of relative strengths and weaknesses. Customization entails nurturing and building on strengths rather than trying to eliminate weaknesses (which is usually impossible). Great firms and outstanding professionals recognize this fact and work with it.

They don't force superlative producers to become indifferent managers. Nor do they penalize highly regarded mentors for devoting time to young stars. On the contrary, they encourage their senior people so that over time their career paths and the performance criteria to which they're held become more individualized. The rewards of this approach are not only more satisfied and productive senior stars but also a firm with a more diversified and balanced portfolio of skills.

Customization requires emphasizing some skills and neglecting others. Assignments that divide a partner's time equally between client and firm responsibilities will nurture his management skills. Pointing a partner toward marketing and client development will foster her skills as a rainmaker. Encouraging a partner to develop intellectual property may produce a guru. The tradeoffs inherent in how professionals allocate their time are inescapable. Taken as a whole, those tradeoffs will determine the likelihood of each individual's success in the partnership, as well as the success of the partnership overall. That is why in professional firms, the deployment of talent is inherently *strategic*.

Strategic Deployment: Connecting Stars to Strategy

All the positive feedback in the world won't make a stitch of difference to professionals who are bored or unhappy with their work. What professionals do—the clients they serve every day, the problems they solve, the colleagues they work with or lead—is where they learn and grow. They may tolerate less-than-satisfying assignments for a while. But over time, if they're just not having any fun they'll leave (or "quit" on the job and underperform). That's why deployment—putting the right person in the right job at the right time—is the most powerful lever a firm has for retaining, motivating, and developing senior stars at every stage of their careers.

Decisions about partner deployment answer two simple questions: Whom do I work for and with? and How do I divide my time between producing and managing? The first question encompasses all the particulars of client assignments. What sort of business or industry are they in? Where are they located? What are the issues they're facing? Have I worked with them before or are they new to the firm (or to me)? The second question addresses the mix of client and management responsibilities each partner assumes. For most the mix will be weighted heavily—if not entirely—toward serving clients. For some, firm responsibilities will come to occupy as much as half or three-quarters of their time.

Beneath these simple questions, however, lies a not-so-simple tension: the tension between the personal desires and needs of the partners and the strategic needs of the firm. If the firm's strategy calls for building a new practice in health care, for example, some of its best and brightest will have to devote time, which could go to established clients, to learning the industry and developing new contacts. If they won't, or if their commitment is half-hearted, nothing much will happen. The firm will have a plan, but not a strategy. Similar dynamics play out around appointments to formal management positions. If someone who has never expressed interest in anything other than client work is made an office head, no one should be surprised if that office doesn't get very much management attention.

On average, PSFs do a better job of deploying stars against client opportunities than they do at meeting their own internal needs. Several factors account for the imbalance. The most immediate is economics. Client loyalty drives the firm's bonus pool, after all, and clients are seldom shy about letting professionals know what (or whom) they need to be satisfied. Second, client assignments are more likely to address a star's professional development needs than an opportunity to get involved in the firm's recruiting process or serve on the compensation committee. If a senior star wants to develop expertise in working with large multinationals, for instance, she may not be crazy about moving to Frankfurt or Tokyo, but she'll certainly understand the rationale. Third and most important, most PSFs don't do as well deploying stars to meet internal needs as they do to meet client needs because they apply the wrong criteria when making internal deployment decisions—specifically management appointments.

In many PSFs, people are chosen as office heads, practice leaders, or regional directors solely on the basis of their client work. Management positions are a reward for client proficiency. The firm may get lucky and discover that one of its star producers is also capable of developing young people or adjudicating the competing demands of fellow partners. But the odds that the assignment will be a mismatch are high for a couple of reasons. One is a compensation system that gets in the way because it's geared toward serving clients and producing current-year revenues or because it rewards titles rather than management results and thus gives partners the wrong incentives for accepting the positions in the first place. The other is the psychology common to many stars, who derive enormous satisfaction and recognition from solving clients' problems and little—if any—from dealing with administrative issues and people problems. Imagine the best software engineer at a firm like IBM Consulting, who derives supreme satisfaction from solving one technical puzzle after another and happens to be the most productive professional in the office, being chosen to coordinate the other engineers rather than work on his own project. If he's forced to take that personally unattractive role, chances are high he would become a turnover candidate. Or he would become so miserable that the other engineers he was supposed to be leading would begin to look for better opportunities.

Managerial shortfalls can easily get lost in the shuffle. Client assignments that are misfiring usually cause considerable noise in the system sooner rather than later, so they tend to be self-correcting. But when young stars leave because they can't stand the partner they're working for, the firm won't be likely to get that feedback unless it actively seeks it out. Absent performance management mechanisms like the exit interviews we mentioned previously, all that the firm will hear is that "this new opportunity was just too good to pass up." In addition, a firm may well be generating solid financial results at the same time that it's losing its most talented professionals—and its future. (The defections may actually contribute to a bigger bottom line in the short run.) Only in the longer term, when the firm looks in vain for the stars to sustain its prosperity and growth, will the problem become apparent. By then it's too late.

Unfortunately, market feedback from clients and colleagues isn't nearly as reliable a guide in making deployment decisions involving senior stars as it is for younger people. Probably just about every PSF has its version of the senior partner who was responsible for three major engagements, all going well. The clients were paying promptly. The junior partners assigned to the projects were doing great work. From the market perspective, everything looked fine. Then the senior partner left. Although no clients applauded the departure, no one was broken-hearted either. It turned out that what the clients valued and were actually buying was the work of the junior partners. As for the junior partners, they didn't decamp (as they probably would have if they hadn't gotten out from under their senior colleague's thumb). Their work was better than ever. And both their motivation and income soared.

Even the more sophisticated young technology companies we studied had an effective mechanism for matching their stars with assignments that maximize their ability to create value, for the firm and for themselves. Cysive, for example, hires mostly engineers who are already experienced in their field. Its leaders try to ensure that the firm runs at a 75 percent to 85 percent utilization range, which they think creates an optimal environment for keeping their professionals challenged but balanced.

Engineers who are not staffed on projects are rotated into this "technology pipeline"—which is essentially a development function, to keep their energy levels up and help them stay on the cutting edge of their field. As Jeff Franco, Cysive's director of operations, explained, "Deployment is very important. Are they doing something that they enjoy? Engineers want to have a problem to solve, but they don't want to be told how to do it. It's the worst conundrum to deal with in each project."

The specifics of a firm's mechanism for deploying resources aren't particularly important. What is important is that it has buy-in from all the partners and reinforces the culture of the firm.

In firms that are still led by their founders, deployment is often despotic: The founder simply "tells" everyone else what to do. After the founders retire, however, or—if they're wise—while they're still active, the firm needs to develop a process for making these decisions.

At Diamond Cluster, for example, cofounders Mel Bergstein (now CEO) and Chris Moffit (now senior VP, secretary, and director) have already distanced themselves from deployment decisions. Staff teams— groups of twelve to fifteen associates and principals who work on a common project—are assigned and managed by partners, who are also charged with the team members' career development.

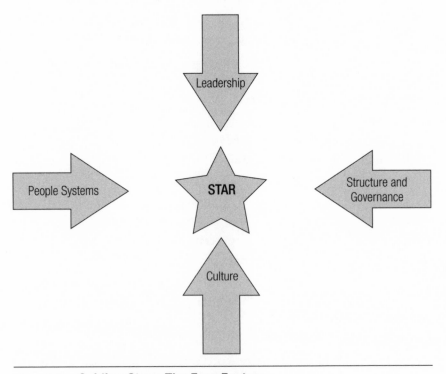

Figure 5-2   **Guiding Stars: The Four Factors**

Deployment decisions involve a constant balancing act between what's right for the firm and what's right for the individual star. At the end of the day, the decisions have to work on both dimensions *and* the stars need to feel that over time their needs come first. Nothing can make the balancing act disappear. But the continuing stream of information performance management provides (about individual partner's goals and dreams as well as the many facets of their performance) can make balancing more manageable by keeping the firm in touch with its stars and the stars in touch with the firm.

Well-designed, effectively implemented people systems are a critical factor in guiding the behavior of individual stars. Critical but insufficient. Aligning partner-level stars—motivating them to perform to their full potential, while generally putting the interests of the firm first—requires not only first-rate people systems but also reinforcement from the firm's structure and governance (its formal organization), its culture, and its institutional leadership (see figure 5-2). In the next three chapters, we will look at how each of these factors contributes to a firm's ability to align its stars.

6 ★ Organization

Aligning Stars and Strategy

HOW SHOULD a professional service firm organize to achieve its strategic goals in a fast-changing and tumultuous business environment? The question is straightforward. The answer is anything but.

In most manufacturing and service companies (and most management texts), strategy leads and organization follows. Decisions about who reports to whom and how the organization will be structured follow closely on the heels of new strategic choices. The implementation may not be seamless, but there's no question about whether the CEO can redraw the organization chart, reengineer the company, or spin off an underperforming unit based on his judgment of what needs to happen. In PSFs, this neat cause-and-effect relationship falls apart. Decisions about organization and strategy go hand in hand—and often it's the organization that leads, while the firm's strategy limps along behind.

What makes PSFs *different*? In traditional corporations, power is essentially positional and top-down, while financial success depends heavily on the efficacy of the company's operations, marketing, and distribution activities and on the systems and organization that shape them. In PSFs, power is attached to individuals as well as to positions. Professionals derive power from their accomplishments and expertise: Peers and younger professionals will respect you and follow your lead if you are outstanding at your craft and effective with clients, regardless of your formal position in the firm. Even senior leaders are likely to allow you to follow your instincts. As a result, power and influence are more widely distributed among the partners of a PSF than they are in a typical, large corporation with a more rigid, hierarchical structure. The better the performance and capabilities of the senior group, the wider the distribution of power reaches.

Equally important, the quality and productivity of this senior group is what drives the PSF's business model. Where manufacturing companies can rely on a production line or a distribution system, PSFs are dependent on the capabilities and motivation of their senior stars. If these highly paid, relatively independent men and women can't—or won't—implement a new strategic direction defined by the firm's most senior leaders, the strategy, however clever, is irrelevant.

Think back to the set of specific strategic choices we discussed in chapter 3. Can a firm *make* its partners pursue certain types of clients at the expense of others? Or make them stop working on low-margin projects for clients with whom they have long-standing relationships? Or tell them to hand off these long-standing personal clients to colleagues? In a word, No. The same answer applies to business-line decisions: Can the firm make an individual partner cross-sell services if she feels too busy or too uninformed to do so? To geographic choices: Can the firm make a star partner move to another continent if he, his wife, and his teenage children think it's a bad idea? And to pricing decisions: Can the firm dictate the fees quoted to a given client? Firmwide management can try to jam the implementation of such strategic choices down the throats of its senior stars, but the only thing this is likely to do is demotivate them (unless, of course, it provokes them to leave altogether).

Nevertheless, in the best PSFs, there is alignment between the senior stars' behavior and the firm's strategic goals. Individuals, on average, *do* adjust what might be perceived as their own self-interest to join their colleagues in enabling the firm to achieve its goals. They put the firm first. That is why enduring firms endure. The challenge is not a new one, nor is there magic to mastering it. The capacity to align stars and strategy, year after year, depends on the firm's culture and leadership (which we'll look at in the next two chapters) and its organization, broadly defined.

When we use the term *organization*, we have considerably more in mind than the number of offices a firm maintains, or the way professional work is divided into practice areas, or the intricacies of its reporting structure. Properly understood, *organization* encompasses a set of critical choices that every firm must make: About how it will attract, develop, evaluate, and reward its people (the "people systems" we examined in chapters 4 and 5). About its management structure. And about its governance, including the form and distribution of its ownership. On a day-to-day basis, these choices can surface as seemingly discrete and independent decisions. In fact, they are closely connected, and decisions made along one dimension sooner or later reverberate along the others. That is why PSFs are more successful in aligning their stars and strategies when their leaders approach these choices systemically, as parts of a larger, integrated whole. (See figure 6-1.)

Partnerships

Historically, PSFs were biased toward alignment—not because their leaders were thinking consciously about the concept, but because the firms' customary structure promoted it. For centuries, partnership was the only form of organization available to independent contributors who wished to band together in the pursuit of professional success. And historically, professional firms (in the United States and

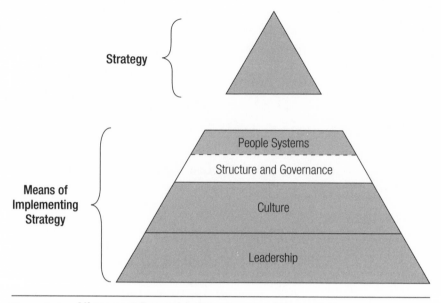

Figure 6-1   Alignment Pyramid: Structure and Governance

elsewhere) were firmly wedded to the general partnership tradition (as law and accounting firms still are).

Even as alternative legal structures such as incorporation evolved and a mix of financial, legal, and tax considerations led many firms to move from legal partnerships to some form of private incorporation, most professional firms continued to *think* of themselves as partnerships. Although their formal structures might be changing, they wanted to retain the *spirit* of partnership because they understood that its allure didn't lie in its tax implications or other legal details. What gave partnership its power (and still does) is a sense of shared destiny, the belief that "we're all in this together, no matter what." Benjamin Franklin articulated the principle in 1776, when he reminded his fellow patriot rebels: "We must indeed all hang together or, most assuredly, we shall all hang separately."

What made the partnership structure so useful for PSFs was that it fostered alignment between the professionals and the organization and strategy of the firm. It achieved this complex alignment, almost unconsciously, and it was able to do so for two important reasons.

First, in a partnership structure, all the partners were owners of the firm. Individually, of course, they made different contributions and held different stakes, but institutionally, they were equal. No partner was a superior or subordinate to any other partner. In other words, the leaders and experienced professionals of the firm were *peers*.

The second important aspect of the structure was that decisions about the firm were made by *all* the partners. At one time the partners probably sat around a table and debated with each other. But even as firms outgrew their tables, and the practice of participation changed or became less intimate, it remained an integral piece of partnership. Decisions might be made by a designated leader in a corner office, just as they would be in a large corporation, but they were still ratified by the partners. These strong *participatory processes* are the second reason partnership was so well suited to PSFs.

Today, partnership is under siege. Not just the structure of partnership, but even the *spirit* of partnership that so many firms have tried to retain. Less than a decade ago, most U.S. PSFs looked similar. The great majority of service providers functioned entirely within the United States, some with a few overseas branches. Whether they were advertising agencies or law firms, information technology specialists or executive search firms, they were mostly private partnerships of manageable size growing organically rather than through acquisitions. Even among successful firms, the mindset was mostly "let's keep doing what we're doing." To the extent there was a "strategy," it was "more of the same." Why not? It had been working well.

That rather orderly world has disappeared. Within the past decade, more and more best-of-breed firms have decided to expand their service offerings and to become international, if not truly global. Most of those firms are growing through acquisitions and mergers as well as through more rapid internal expansion. The new PricewaterhouseCoopers has 9,000 partners. How does a firm of that size preserve the individual partners' feeling of being invested in the organization and the belief that what they think can influence the firm's future direction and success?

Many PSFs that can do so legally have also been making radical changes in their ownership. (Accounting and law firms in the United

States cannot have public ownership.) Some have gone public or have merged or been acquired by other firms, both public and private. In our sample of eighteen firms alone, there were four IPOs and four major combinations (mergers or acquisitions) in the five years we have been studying them.

What happens to a firm like Alex Brown, one of the oldest partnerships in the United States, when it gets acquired by Bankers Trust (in 1997), a public company, and a year later becomes part of a large German bank (Deutsche Bank)? What do these drastic ownership changes do to the principles of partnership that had been cultivated for almost two centuries at Alex Brown? The scope of the changes is difficult to appreciate.

The trends of growing scale and changing ownership put enormous pressure on the principles and practices of partnership. How do you make a decision to change your compensation structure, or replace your chief executive, in a manner that allows individual partners to feel vested in the firm's future when you have 2,000 partners instead of 200 and when they are scattered around the world instead of only in North America? How do you deal with the transparency—and second-guessing—that accompany public ownership? The pressures for quarterly earnings and growth?

It is far too early to tell whether such moves will destroy the *spirit* of partnership at these and other firms or whether the benefits of such moves will outweigh the liabilities. But whatever the outcomes, the game has irrevocably changed throughout the world of professional service. It takes only a few moves by some leading firms to change the competitive dynamics for everyone else in the industry. Hambrecht & Quist insisted for a long time that it wanted to stay independent. Then, in 1999, it allowed itself to be acquired by Chase to gain access to more capital and improve its competitive position. Did the fact that Alex Brown became part of Deutsche Bank influence H&Q's decision? Or Goldman Sachs's 1998 IPO, which also put pressure on competitors whose pockets weren't so deep? Maybe. Maybe not.

What can PSFs do as they grow, merge, or become public? They must make decisions about their structure and governance that reinforce as much as possible the two essential attributes that partnership has always created: *peer relationships* and *participatory processes*.

Networks of Peers

There isn't an organization in the world that doesn't have some element of hierarchy. It is the underlying architecture for all sorts of religious, educational, and government organizations and, of course, for businesses. Ask the CEO of any big manufacturing or service company for a description of the organization and you're likely to get an elaborate chart, filled with lines and boxes arranged in a hierarchical fashion. For more than 100 years, the prevailing wisdom about organizing work has been to create a hierarchy. Divide the work into units; put someone at the head of each; and then rank the unit heads in a chain of command, with everyone reporting to a boss higher up until you reach the CEO. Hierarchy is in the Bible and the records of humankind's earliest civilizations. Even primate societies are hierarchical, as biologists and zoologists continually remind us.

Given how deeply rooted in human experience the concept of hierarchy is, it isn't surprising that we find it in PSFs too. But while hierarchy may be a great model for manufacturing companies and other businesses, it's a poor fit for talent-driven organizations (a fact that many traditional, multitiered companies are in the process of discovering as they become more dependent on knowledge workers). It is especially awkward in PSFs, where command and control are incompatible with the professional work required to serve clients, as well as with the psyches of the professionals themselves.

Fading Hierarchies

While no PSF that we know of has abandoned hierarchy entirely, the most successful firms limit the height of their pyramids and try to create a flatter structure that reinforces the sense of governing through a partnership of peers. The leaders of these firms are among the first to downplay hierarchy's importance. Steve Pfeiffer, of Fulbright & Jaworski, spoke for his peers in the study group in pointing out that "we don't have a lot of hierarchy, and we don't have a lot of bureaucracy."

Even larger firms like Ernst & Young, which, because of their size, inevitably have more levels of hierarchy and a more top-down form of governance, make efforts to preserve a partnership atmosphere. They solicit input from their partners, using representative democracy through committees of partners to keep them involved in decisions. They also make an effort to build consensus before decisions are made. Phil Laskawy, chairman and CEO, says, "Some outside observers would say that we have a hierarchical structure. But the reality is we have a more democratic process than most of these firms. We accomplish this by keeping our partners and personnel informed, and getting all partners to recognize that their input is important. What they say really counts. These are important elements of what makes this firm work, even though partners don't vote on every issue."

Because the management structures in these firms have only a few levels, and the trend is toward reducing their number rather than letting them grow, they are most aptly described as *fading hierarchies*. As Kelly O'Dea, worldwide president of client services at Ogilvy & Mather, explained, "The organization here is flatter than it was five, six, or seven years ago. Far flatter." In addition, what in other contexts would be called the "corporate office" is purposely kept as small as possible. Equally telling, in many firms, "headquarters" isn't necessarily where the CEO is located. When John Donahoe became the chief executive of Bain, for example, he stayed in San Francisco and the firm's headquarters remained in Boston. Similarly, when Rajat Gupta was elected managing partner of McKinsey, he stayed in Chicago and the firm's headquarters remained in New York City.

A Different Kind of Matrix

The phrase that comes up most often when professionals describe their firm's structure is "matrix" organization. Although the details vary, each of the firms in our study is structured as a matrix with relatively fixed dimensions, which provides the firm's management skeleton, and a dynamic dimension, which changes to meet clients' needs. The matrix's fixed dimensions are the firm's management structure at any given time, including the geographic offices and professional practice areas that provide "homes" for the professionals: the New Delhi office of an advertising agency, say, or the intellectual property practice of a law firm. The partners who occupy the formal leadership positions in this portion of the matrix usually have some client responsibilities, but they are chiefly responsible for ensuring the health of the stars in their units and the economic success of the unit overall.

The variable portion of the matrix consists of client teams, which are always works in progress. Every time a project is completed, or a client relationship ends, the professionals engaged in that work are redeployed. Even in fields (such as accounting and advertising) in which long-term relationships with clients are customary, the professionals move frequently from one project to another and work on several simultaneously. As a result, the firm faces a constant stream of decisions about whom to assign where and whose activities will have to be integrated with whose.

Because a matrix blends the management side of the firm with the client-oriented side, it can facilitate these critical deployment decisions (as well as ensure the effective implementation of the people systems). Facilitate but not resolve. The matrices in PSFs differ from their counterparts in corporations (where the form originated) in two respects that make the work of managing them especially challenging. First, there is no common boss with the positional power to resolve conflicts. In traditional corporations, the matrices basically consist of at least two hierarchies, one vertical, the other horizontal, which report to a single executive. Subordinates lower down in the hierarchy resolve most issues themselves because passing decisions up the line is frowned on. But the fact that there is a common boss "up there" contributes to the pressure for timely resolution.

In PSFs, such hierarchical power to force decisions among the dimensions is limited. If an office head and a practice leader disagree about the expertise required on a particular client project or about the assignment that will best develop a young star, there's no "boss" to whom they can easily refer the decision. To resolve issues and get collaboration across the firm's many units, therefore, leaders and professionals alike have to develop the skills to resolve differences and the commitment to do what will serve the firm's interest best.

The other distinction between corporate and PSF matrices is that the structure of the latter is always in flux. Change is constant, even in such relatively stable units as geographic offices and industry practices, because the constellations of stars within these units are primarily defined by clients' needs, and those needs are a moving target. Dan Case, the chairman and CEO of Hambrecht & Quist, described some of the changes in his firm's structure. "Once upon a time, there was one investment-banking department. Now there is Technology, and Health Care, and Branded Consumer Products, and inside Technology there's a software group, and an Internet group, and so on. We keep breaking these things into smaller areas, smaller vertical industry groups."

Further complicating the work of coordination are the many small teams that form monthly—if not weekly—around client projects. As teams disperse and regroup, both the cast of decision makers and the responsibilities of particular individuals shift. In addition, since professionals often work with more than one team simultaneously, it's not uncommon for a partner to be "reporting to" a colleague on one project while taking the lead on another. So there's little opportunity to develop the kind of stability in roles and relationships that facilitates decision making and conflict resolution in traditional matrices. Professionals not only have to learn to work with new counterparts quickly but also have to be able to look at problems from new and different perspectives.

The omnipresence of challenges like these is what makes performance-measurement and reward systems that reinforce partnership behavior such an integral part of a PSF's organization. As you saw in chapter 5, the best systems track results on three dimensions to encourage collaboration and teamwork: the individual's personal performance, the performance of his or her unit, and the performance of the entire firm. What this comes down to, in the words of Patrick Pittard, Heidrick & Struggles's CEO, is "one very important criterion, which has got heavy weight and can hit you in the pocketbook: partnership. Do you work in teams and do you invite other people into your clients?"

The matrix structure in PSFs also contributes to a form of governance that is effective and essential in managing senior professionals because it reinforces the sense of peer relationships. Partners have to work things out themselves. There is no "kicking it up to the next level" to resolve a conflict or to make a decision. Whatever their formal titles, therefore, in the final analysis "partners" are colleagues, not superiors or subordinates.

Limited Management Tenure

The policies that govern individuals' appointment to and tenure in management positions further reinforce peer relationships. The most conspicuous, of course, is the fact that management positions are almost all part-time: With the possible exception of the managing partner or CEO and other members of his leadership team, everyone is a producing manager. Second, leaders in many positions must be endorsed by their partners either formally or informally. Finally, senior stars rotate into—and out of—management and committee assignments on a regular basis. Limited tenure through term limits and rotation ensures that partners manage and lead the firm together, as a group of peers.

Ernst & Young's U.S. partnership, for instance, elects a partner advisory council composed of eighteen members that is responsible for ratifying the management committee's selection of the chairman of the firm as well as the chairman's selection of the members of the management committee. It also ratifies any merger that increases the firm's revenues by more than 5 percent and any partnership agreement changes. The members of the council serve staggered three-year terms, with one third of the council turning over each year.

Skadden Arps, to cite another example, has several committees comprising both rotating members, who are selected from the partners via a nomination process, and members who serve by virtue of their position at the firm. The policy committee, for example, is chaired by Robert Sheehan, executive partner, and made up of thirteen members who serve staggered five- and four-year terms, plus two legal practice partners (one from the firm's corporate side, the other from litigation). Sheehan and the two legal practice partners also serve ex officio on the compensation committee, which has eight rotating members, and the financial-oversight committee, which has three rotating members.

Together, these organizational choices create structures that can best be described as networks of peers. The elaborate hierarchical organization charts that map the reporting relationships in most companies have no analog in the flat structures of PSFs. Peers are not necessarily equals: Some partners hold larger ownership stakes than others, or deliver more outstanding performances year to year, or provide better counsel to their partners and younger staff. But despite these differences, the mindset is basically democratic—"we're all partners here." So for all the healthy competition among partners, in the best firms there is an equally healthy measure of collaboration and cooperation in the interest of the firm.

The Power of Participation

Historically, partnership has done more than define the structure and ownership of a firm. Its democratic bias has also affected how professional organizations deal with governance issues. *Governance* answers the questions, "How are the senior stars involved in significant firmwide decisions?" "In what decisions do they become involved?" and "How are such decisions made?" In some firms, this bias goes so far as to mandate a "one partner, one vote" approach to all critical decisions. But even where the democracy isn't quite so literal and extensive, the notion of participation, of actively involving senior stars who don't occupy formal management positions (as well as those who do) in key decisions is firmly ingrained in the governance processes.

Here, again, the contrast with traditional corporate practice—where decisions are wired in from the top, down, and everyone knows who the decision makers are—is dramatic. In a traditional company, if someone steps out of line and oversteps the authority of her position, she will hear about it quickly and forcefully. But that approach won't wash when the company's key revenue producers are also independent partners with the ability to directly influence firm profits—or to leave and hang out their own shingles. Senior stars expect to be consulted, not only on matters vital to the firm's future but also on the myriad day-to-day decisions that affect them personally. If they are not, they will voice their dissatisfaction or show it by moving toward the door. By necessity, therefore, the governance of professional organizations has to be more inclusive and participatory. That's why the partnership form worked so well. And why even where it is coming under pressure, firms must continue to reinforce the participatory nature that made (and continues to make) the principle and spirit of partnership so persistent.

While informal participation is a hallmark of many well-managed companies and typically takes place on an ad hoc basis, "partnership-like" organizations establish formal processes to involve their senior stars in critical governance issues. What's a critical issue? Anything that will vitally affect the organization's future. Across the board in the firms we studied, a handful of decisions fell into this category: decisions about the organization's long-term strategy, about its ownership form (whether to go public, merge, acquire, or be acquired), about admitting new partners and distributing the wealth (dividing the pie), and about choosing new leadership, especially the firmwide leader. For such decisions, the particulars of the process the firm uses are less significant than the fact that the partners have confidence in it and support the outcome. We saw this earlier in chapter 5, when we examined promotion and compensation processes (although we didn't label them as "governance" decisions). Here, as a further example, we'll consider one of the most unusual aspects of PSF governance—the selection of the managing partner or CEO.

Choosing Your Own "CEO"

Can you imagine the senior management of GE voting on the next CEO? Or the line management of GM initiating leadership change? Hardly. Yet that's what happens in outstanding PSFs. There are significant differences among their practices, as we'll see. But in each case, the succession process works. Every organization in our original research group has gone through a successful leadership transition at least once, and most have gone through several. (In fact, the capacity to bring in a new leader, at least once, was one of the criteria we used to select the eighteen best-in-class organizations we initially studied.)

The selection of a new leader is an emotion-filled event, not only for the candidates but also for the firm. Everybody cares deeply about who gets chosen and how because everyone knows that the choice will influence the direction of his or her career as well as the success of the firm. Too much emotion can fray the firm's cohesiveness, and too many disappointed candidates—and their supporters—can compromise the new leader's ability to lead. So whatever methods a firm uses, the partners must perceive them to be fair and rational, focused on objective factors tied directly to the needs of the firm. In addition, the successful candidate has to have the support of a substantial majority of the firm's stars. He or she can't just sneak in by a few votes.

Some firms, especially those that have kept a partnership- or private-corporate form of ownership, satisfy these objectives through a formal election process. Everyone knows who the candidates are, and the candidates, in turn, make their positions on firmwide issues known, so that all the partners can become informed before casting their votes. At Fulbright & Jaworski, for example, "the leader is elected by everybody, . . . with a secret ballot and KPMG doing all the counting, so no one knows where the power base is." Similarly, at Heidrick & Struggles, nominees write position papers and give speeches as part of an election process in which one person at a time drops out, and "usually someone gets a majority before it gets down to two candidates."

The process is more indirect in larger partnerships such as Ernst & Young. As Bill Kimsey, deputy chairman and COO, says, "Twenty-five hundred partners can't, through listening to campaign speeches, figure out who the chairman should be. It's not a beauty contest." It's also more indirect in firms that are publicly held or parts of larger public entities. Shelly Lazarus, the CEO of Ogilvy & Mather, was appointed by Sir Martin Sorrel, the chairman of parent company WPP, for example. Nevertheless, as she explains, her appointment "had to be approved by many other people. This company is a highly interdependent matrix . . . and all the dimensions had to come into play. So it is a democracy in this regard, because anyone could have stopped it along the way."

Even Goldman Sachs, whose succession process one partner likened to "a hummingbird—it shouldn't fly but it does," incorporated objectivity and a certain amount of democracy into what were, historically at least, somewhat autocratic decisions. A partner with a long memory remembers hearing that "when Gus Levy died, he left it in his will that John Weinberg and John Whitehead should be the next senior partners." But "they were clearly the people, there was no doubt about that."

The process became less top-down thereafter, when the firm's management committee took it over. But even so, Hank Paulson, the current CEO, and others could honestly claim that, when they were younger, they weren't bothered by the fact that they didn't have a say in who the senior partners would be. Why were they so sanguine? They were confident that the committee members would act in the firm's best interest: that choosing someone who was unacceptable to the partnership would be unthinkable because it would risk an awkward—and therefore potentially harmful—ratifying vote.

A Professional Democracy

Much like the U.S. Congress, PSFs work through a committee structure, which provides the primary mechanism for involving partners in major decisions. The names and functions of the committees vary among firms, as do the methods for selecting their members. In some firms, committee members are elected. In others, the firm's leader appoints them. And in others still, they're selected by some combination of the two methods. What's common—and crucial—is that regardless of how they're chosen, the members of these committees merit their colleagues' respect and trust. The words that one management consultant used to describe the members of his firm's compensation committee summed up a view we heard repeatedly: "The most trusted and least apparently self-interested partners are on [it]. There is a set of decision rules, but within that there are judgments. At the end of the day, it is a very trusted committee [and] that seems to work."

Accomplished stars expect and are expected to participate, from time to time, on one or another of their firm's committees. In addition to giving partners a voice in shaping the firm, these committees serve as an important vehicle for building consensus. If the members of a committee make a decision or agree to a proposal from the firm's leader, they can become its ambassadors with their associates throughout the firm.

McKinsey recently finished a strategy development process lasting a year and a half that intimately involved every partner in the firm. A task force of seventy partners selected by Rajat Gupta, the managing partner, designed the initiative, and together the rest of the partnership, including alumni of the firm, participated in a series of workshops to discuss, evaluate, and refine the firm's strategy.

"We had a dialogue together," Rajat Gupta told us. "Everybody now understands why different people think differently, whether it's a result of their immediate environment or whether it's the position in the life cycle of where they are in their careers, or their position about the particular client they are serving and what's happening in their industries. There's a much greater understanding and tolerance, even appreciation, of the diversity of the firm."

The process resulted in a series of new initiatives. One is a guiding principle McKinsey calls "100 percent Cubed," which means the firm is committed to delivering 100 percent of the firm, 100 percent of the time, in 100 percent of the world. As a result of the iterative, inclusive process, all of the partners "own" the idea and have a personal stake in its success in their specific offices, teams, and individual work within the firm. The key was that each partner felt involved and contributed.

Committees also help spread the work of governing the firm. In a world of time-pressed producing managers, the old adage "many hands make light work" is apt. The way Bob Hallagan, vice chairman and former CEO of Heidrick & Struggles, describes the firm's approach to its committee structure is representative: "When driving a firm like a partnership, people must be led not managed. At Heidrick & Struggles we first painted a future vision of the firm that everyone was excited about. Once we gained their enthusiasm, we broke the vision down into absolute key success drivers and established committees to drive the programs. The committees get everyone involved and feeling part of the success."

Last but hardly least, the fact that these committees exist creates a counterweight to the power of the firm's leadership. A partner at McKinsey explained the logic: "The line organization is the managing director and the office heads, but committees elected by the partnership are there to be a sort of check-and-balance that promotions and partner compensation are all done fairly and equitably, and that the right decisions are made." In the event that the firm's leader or those she appoints to leadership jobs misuse their positions, or move in directions that are inconsistent with the views of their partners, the committee structure provides a remedy. Perhaps most important, the mere existence of these committees reminds each firm's leader that it is a democracy—that his power ultimately rests on the support of his partner-peers.

Committees aren't the only sign of democratic process, however. Formal partnership votes on issues such as admission to the partnership, leadership succession, or a change in the firm's form of ownership are also common. Often such votes are required by the partnership agreement or the firm's bylaws. But the leaders of these organizations also have to develop a sixth sense about what should be put to a vote. The reason: Only a small proportion of the senior stars can serve on a committee at any given time, and yet everyone expects to be informed about and involved in major issues nevertheless. As Hank Paulson, CEO at Goldman Sachs, put it, "We'd vote on anything big, whatever that means, and we'd all know it when we saw it. . . . We'd rather not define it and we haven't bureaucratized any of that stuff."

In addition, most of these firms, if practical, hold periodic meetings of all the partners to discuss major issues, facilitate communication, and, perhaps most important, strengthen the bonds among them. The most unusual of these retreats may be the weeklong meetings McKinsey held in Portugal in 1996 for partners and their spouses. The assignment: Write and produce an opera. Were they trying to improve the musical abilities of the partnership? Not really. The goal was to build personal ties and reinforce the sense that "we're all partners here."

Executives who have spent their careers in traditional corporations would doubtless find these meetings and committees a source of frustration and irritation. Not the leaders of these firms, who know what's involved in sustaining partnerships. They understand that the governance system gives them a set of tools to work with, and they use the committee structure to help build consensus. Beyond this, they spend countless hours talking one on one with the firm's senior stars to understand their perspectives and to discuss issues on which they want their support. Phrases like *working issues, building coalitions to support initiatives,* and *two steps forward, one step back,* which pepper their conversation, reflect their appreciation for the subtleties of democratic leadership.

The Dark Side of Participation

Up till now, we've been talking about participation as if it were an unalloyed positive. It's not, as anyone with experience in a highly participatory organization knows all too well. Broad participation in decision making and consensus building slows decisions down. It also can make it difficult to reach a definitive conclusion. Imagine, for example, that your firm has decided to expand into Europe, which means moving senior stars and resources out of existing U.S. offices and into new ones (and persuading a number of experienced stars to move). The partners in those existing offices are unlikely to say "No dice." That would be uncollegial. They are likely to drag their feet, however, and say, "Sorry, but we simply can't cannibalize this office for the sake of a new one in

Frankfurt or London or Milan." Getting them to agree will take time. If they really dig in their heels, it may lead to the abandonment of the idea. It just doesn't seem to be worth the effort to overcome their passive resistance.

Participation can also diffuse responsibility. If everyone is in charge, no one's in charge. In PSFs whose leaders are overly deferential to their partners' views, the decision-making process often seizes up. Unless a firm has leaders who, when necessary, will assert themselves and use their influence to press for action, the only decisions it's likely to make are decisions not to decide. Peter Georgescu, who recently retired as CEO of Young & Rubicam, summarized the leader's dilemma brilliantly: "I have knee pads and a 45," he said. "I get down and beg a lot, but I shoot people, too." In other words, persuasion and developing consensus are essential, but so is pressing for action, and at some point stragglers have to be prodded into line.

Although leaders of PSFs don't have the positional power and authority of corporate CEOs, they do have ammunition for the 45s they need to carry. First and foremost is their personal skill and expertise. Professional abilities and success with clients are an important criterion in selecting someone to become the leader of a firm. The new leader may not be the absolute best accountant, banker, or consultant, but she will be admired for her professional accomplishments, and they will be an important source of her ongoing influence. Professionals at Skadden Arps didn't follow Joe Flom because he sat in a corner office. They followed him because they respected his skill and success as a lawyer.

The fact that firm leaders are selected through processes that their colleagues accept as legitimate also strengthens their hand. Partners are more likely to follow their lead because they have agreed that this is the person they want to lead them. Direction from the center is unlikely to be resisted—as long as the firm is prospering, and its stars are enjoying their work. Let firm results turn sour, though, and the leader's ideas and initiatives will be scrutinized and challenged. Power can evaporate quickly, which is why interpersonal skills—the ability to listen and to understand others' points of view, to persuade others that a new direction makes sense, and to stay the course—are so extraordinarily important, not just to the leader's success but also to the firm's. We shall expand on this in chapter 8.

Structure, Governance, and Ownership: The "New" Bain & Company, Inc.

In 1990, Bain & Company initiated a complex ownership transition from its small founding group to a broadly diversified global partnership. The course of this management buy-out led the partnership to implement an integrated array of organizational changes designed to better align the "new" Bain around its ambitious goals. As with most such founder transitions, the process was challenging and cumbersome—but it worked.

Bain & Company had once been labeled "too hot to handle" in a magazine article reflecting the firm's successful hyper-growth through most of the 1980s. In 1988, however, the world's most secretive strategy consulting firm stumbled into view with the early stages of a comprehensive restructuring.

Simply put, Bain had outgrown its organization. Although there were more than fifty "vice presidents," nominally a partner-level title, ownership was concentrated in the hands of seven founders. Vice presidents were largely excluded from strategic decisions and often barely informed after the fact. Four layers separated the CEO from a new vice president, who had no formal way to participate effectively in firm governance. Vice presidents were well paid and aggressively managed, but the *really* big money still flowed to the founding group who controlled the business on a collegial—but top-down—basis. The organization was more like an atom, with a powerful core of founding partners surrounded by subsidiary stars, than a network of peers.

Throughout the 1970s and 1980s, this organizational approach had worked well. The founders were exceptional consultants, and they recruited talented stars excited to be part of an extraordinary team. Then, gradually, years before the restructuring, things started to change. The vice-president group expanded and became more geo-graphically diverse as Bain opened offices around the world. The younger stars' skills and client work began to rival those of the foun-ders (they had, after all, been trained by them); while the founders, on the other hand, were slowing down after decades in the consulting business (and plenty of money in the bank). At some point, the lines crossed. Without anyone realizing it, the vice presidents, as a group, eclipsed the founders. At that undefined moment, Bain's organiza-tional structure and governance, already straining under years of aggressive growth, became an invisible liability.

Today, more than a decade later, the firm is once again a global leader in strategy consulting, with more than 2,700 employees in twenty countries and an array of successful adjacent businesses. Although today partners refer to "old" Bain and "new" Bain as road markers of the firm's transformation, at a distance the "new" Bain looks almost identical to the old version. The vice-president group (absent most of the founders) is essentially the same, although sub-stantially larger. Not a word of the mission statement has changed. The firm's client strategy remains focused on delivering exceptional results to senior management across a broad array of industries. International expansion has continued. Bain's innovative pricing strat-egy (partially equity-based) remains a centerpiece of its practice. Bain people still look, talk, and act like "Bainees," singing along with the Bain Band at off-site meetings.

Nevertheless, beginning in the late 1980s something happened that fundamentally altered the organization and laid the foundation for its reinvigoration. That something was a set of integrated organiza-tional changes that rewired the partnership and ultimately altered the behavior, values, and performance of its senior stars.

First, the old ownership model was scrapped, replaced by a new inclusive partnership. Ownership was extended from the small group of founders to a broad global team that today numbers more than 200 partners. A partner's equity stake provided the basis for participation in the firm's governance. For the first time ever, partners began to debate—and vote on—the central questions facing the partnership. The group elected a new managing partner (chief executive) and a non-executive chairman of the board from among their number. The compensation system was reborn: The partners voted on alternatives (designed to link individual incentives more closely with the firm's strategic goals) proposed by a task force of their peers. Even the firm's historically robust strategy was debated, refined, and ultimately reendorsed by the partnership.

A massive increase in communication augmented this formal participation. The firm's financial statements were shared with the partners for the first time. *Glasnost*—open, honest, and direct communication—emerged as a guiding theme. The first worldwide partner retreat in a decade took place, followed by another that included spouses. People who participated as partner–owners gradually began to feel—and behave—like partner–owners who put the firm's needs ahead of their own. An entirely new approach to governance, designed around the new Bain partnership, reinforced these emerging peer relationships.

Governance was aligned with other organizational elements. The partners elected a policy committee to lead long-term strategy development. A compensation committee was elected to oversee partner compensation and promotion. A nominating committee rode shotgun over the election process for committee members, the chief executive, and the chairman of the board. Every leadership position had term limits, from a minimum of one three-year term on the nominating committee to a maximum of three, three-year terms for the chief executive. The office heads formed regional operating committees, which became the backbone of firm management; and they were expected to return to full-time client work after serving for five to seven years.

The firm's approach to managing its partners' performance was also transformed. Increasingly higher standards that measured both financial and nonfinancial contributions were established for every partner. Partners were evaluated and rewarded on "people asset building," "one-firm behavior," and "knowledge contribution." Peer reviews and upward feedback surveys were instituted. Annual compensation came to depend upon a mix of individual and team contribution rather than on tenure and rank.

Within two years, ownership, governance, organizational structure, and partner performance management were entirely rethought and reconstructed to form a new, integrated whole. Externally, to clients and recruits, Bain looked the same. Internally, a new Bain was born, aligned around a set of new realities.

The particulars of Bain's experience won't be repeated—at least not by Bain. The transition from a founding group to a partnership is complete. What will recur, for Bain and every PSF that wants to survive and prosper, is the challenge of keeping its organization and strategy aligned in the face of aggressive growth, diversification, and intense competitive pressures.

Professional service firms are facing more pressure than ever before. At the same time that the forces that would pull them apart are intensifying, the countervailing forces holding them together are weakening. Growth, globalization, and changes in ownership are undermining the historic partnership structure and challenging the partnership spirit. In such an environment, firms must find a way to nurture the alignment between their stars and the firm's objectives. While organizational decisions that reinforce peer relationships and participation can help, they are useless without the basic underlying belief in these principles of partnership. How can firms maintain this belief and commitment to partnership when so many forces are at work eroding them? Ultimately, the answer lies in their *culture*. A strong culture can weave new strategic and organizational choices together, and hold them in alignment, despite revolutionary pressures, as Bain's transformation attests. A strong culture can also provide enormous help in attracting, retaining, and motivating stars. In the following chapter, we'll look at the down-to-earth ways in which this sometimes amorphous-seeming concept works.

7 ★ Culture

A Force for Alignment

IT'S 2 A.M. *on Sunday in New York, and a partner at a consulting firm is expecting a phone call from a colleague in Tokyo. He's going to be briefing her about a multinational consumer goods company he worked with two years ago. She'll be meeting with the company on Tuesday morning to pitch a long-term project.*

The partner in New York is well prepared for the phone call. He took time on Friday to pull together a package of information—to review his experiences, to synthesize his knowledge. Time away from his current clients. Time away from selling new business. Personal time. For someone in Tokyo he barely knows. There's no rule book that says he has to do this, nor will he get any tangible reward.

The phone call lasts three hours. His colleague is grateful; he's glad he could help. The meeting on Tuesday goes well; the multinational signs on. The firm beats a direct competitor; the cash register rings.

It's 2 A.M. on Sunday in New York, and a partner at another consulting firm is sleeping. A colleague in Tokyo called him last week, asking for advice on a multinational client with whom she knew he had a great deal of experience. He spent fifteen minutes on the phone with her, giving her an overview. He didn't offer to do more; she didn't expect him to do more. Six years ago, he would have taken the time to be more helpful. But that was then; this is now. The firm isn't the same place it once was; it's every man for himself these days.

Two weeks later, the client takes its business elsewhere, saying in a letter that the competitor it has chosen to do business with is "better prepared to handle the needs of a growing, global company." The firm takes an imperceptible step toward mediocrity.

What's the critical difference between these two firms?

In a word: Culture.

Most people believe that culture is amorphous and intangible—something that exists and influences behavior at the margin, but certainly isn't strategic. They also believe that culture is something you inherit, rather than something you create and manage.

They're right—but only to a point. Culture is amorphous; it is intangible. But it *directly* affects the behavior of every single person in your organization. And it isn't simply inherited; it isn't just *there*. To borrow a quote from Shakespeare, "What's past is prologue." Culture is dynamic. And whether you know it or not, you *manage* it on a daily basis. You shape the culture of your firm by the decisions you make or facilitate, which then affect behavior, which subsequently becomes part of "how things are done here." You may be reinforcing the culture you inherited through your actions; you may also be breaking new ground, changing the culture of your firm, slightly or drastically, and significantly affecting your firm's competitive position as you do.

As we've seen, success has a price. Success can bring complexity—a larger firm, for example, and one that is operating all over the world. Success—and growth—can also bring a concomitant need for capital and currency for paying stars, which may lead a private firm to go public. Changes like these inevitably threaten the strategic identity and alignment that have driven the firm's success. But the firms that endure through growing pains, changes in ownership, and other challenges manage their culture to minimize the stress of change. They turn to it as a support mechanism and as a rudder to remind them of their course in the face of new challenges. And they work to change it, as needed, to adapt to new circumstances. (See figure 7-1.)

What's Culture?

Reduced to its essentials, *culture* is a system of beliefs that members of an organization share about the goals and values that are important to them and about the behavior that is appropriate to attain

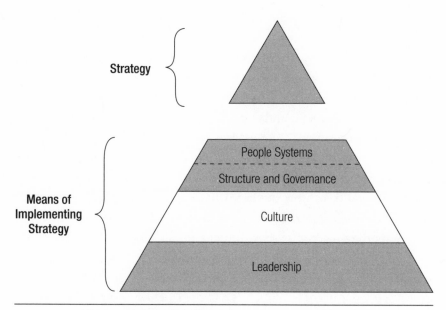

Figure 7-1   **Alignment Pyramid: Culture**

those goals and live those values. The concept of culture had its roots in anthropological studies in the early twentieth century. Social scientists used the term to refer to the persistent pattern of beliefs and customs they observed in their studies of South Pacific islanders, African bush dwellers, and American Indian tribes, among others. Several decades later, scholars interested in business organizations recognized that companies and firms also developed patterns of beliefs and customs, and that those beliefs and customs had a strong influence on how employees behaved. And so the concept was brought into the modern business vocabulary.

Culture encompasses beliefs about everything that goes on in a firm. Culture is never completely codified in a formal rule book or a policy manual. Instead it is a set of invisible guideposts that define how people should behave. It establishes the "dos"—what you are expected to do—and also the "don'ts"—what is implicitly prohibited—at levels ranging from the smallest of decisions (what to wear) to the largest (what line of business the firm is in, or whether to accept a certain client).

At Bain, for example—and this is a small thing, but telling—consultants are obsessive about communicating through voice mail. Messages are sent and received by hundreds of professionals every hour, from sites around the globe. People are expected to check voice mail on Saturdays, Sundays, and even over vacation. The practice isn't recorded in an employee handbook or taught in introductory training sessions. But everyone knows that they must remain connected, in real time, to case teams, colleagues, and clients. Memos are rare in Bain's fast-paced environment, and e-mail, while useful, is only a backup in its highly oral culture.

Hambrecht & Quist provides another good example. At H&Q, seasoned bankers routinely take associates with them to client meetings, spending time after the event to debrief. They explain why they approached the client *this* way. Why they didn't start the meeting *that* way. Why they reacted as they did when the client said *this*. Why they didn't offer *that* information. The practice isn't required by some written policy. It's not part of a formal training program. It's done because that's the way Hambrecht & Quist teaches its junior people the art of client management. It's done because "That's the way we do things here."

There's a tendency on the part of many top managers to believe that they can legislate behavior through edicts and devices such as job descriptions. (Think about the millions of dollars in money and time that have been spent on elaborate new organization charts and job descriptions that are expected to transform people's behavior.) The habit is understandable, given the industrial heritage of business. And in factory settings, where employees punch time clocks and work on assembly lines, it's natural that policy, procedure, and discipline shape behavior even today.

But in PSFs, where people have so much personal discretion and autonomy, culture has more influence on a professional's behavior than any job description or corporate policy ever written. Policies and procedures, manuals, and job descriptions cannot dictate behavior effectively where professionals work without close supervision, people are running their own offices and practices, partners are serving their own clients, and leadership is highly decentralized. Culture is a dominant force—if not *the* dominant force—in determining how the members of the firm actually behave toward one another and toward their clients. The greater the degree of freedom, the more important culture is in determining how an individual works.

Survival of the Culturally Fit

Unfortunately, there are no clear mortality rates for PSFs. Firms are acquired or drift into obscurity. Once-powerful firms falter, restructure, revive, and falter again. Flawed strategic or organizational choices drive much of this failure, yet the root causes often appear to be subtler. What is it about the organization of professionals that allows some firms to adapt to marketplace turmoil and prosper, while others lose share and gradually decline? Why do some firms seem to thrive on change while others melt down?

The answer, we believe, is found in the organization's culture. One reason we chose to study enduring "best-in-class" firms was to see whether cultural attributes contributed to their sustainability and prosperity. The evidence is clear: They do. Much as certain biological traits help species adapt more readily to evolutionary forces, certain cultural beliefs help firms adapt to economic turmoil and change.

Just as a firm's culture guides the decisions its members make, day by day, about the work they perform for clients and their relationships with colleagues, it shapes the ways that they respond to internal and external threats. If a firm's cultural beliefs are well developed along certain crucial dimensions, it is likely to overcome threats to its success and eventually prosper. If those beliefs are underdeveloped or seriously flawed, however, the firm is likely to fail.

While every organization's culture is distinctive and in many ways unique, outstanding firms are remarkably similar in the norms and beliefs that constitute their cultural core. Why the congruence? The explanation lies in the tensions that are an inherent part of every PSF's business model. *Tensions among partners* who are both collegial and competitive, and who constantly vie for a pool of scarce human resources and for the rewards of their efforts. *Tensions within client teams,* which form and reform around specific assignments and provide a breeding ground for conflict at a personal level. Complex *tensions that cut through the entire organization,* as the community wrestles with issues across business lines, functional areas, and parts of the globe. *Tensions between the needs of stars and the demands of clients,* which can play out almost hour by hour. Finally, the perennial *tension between satisfying one generation of partners at the expense of coming generations,* between consuming today or investing for tomorrow.

The further we examined each of the firms in our study, the more evidence we found of the critical role that culture plays in containing these fundamental tensions. In every case, a core of beliefs had evolved within the firm, which helped its members accommodate the tensions endemic to their business. These beliefs did not link neatly to the tensions. It wasn't, and isn't, a matter of matching specific tensions with specific beliefs. Rather, each belief offset some or all of the tensions, more so or less so, depending on the circumstance at hand. These core beliefs guided the firm's behavior through business cycles and generations, exerting a powerful force for cohesion and ensuring their survival.

The Cultural Core

Whether we were looking at accounting firms or information technology companies, advertising agencies or law firms, five core beliefs characterized the way that the senior stars thought about their organization and their own relationship to it: belief in partnership, in extraordinary teams, in community, in stars first/clients first, and in perpetuity (see figure 7-2).

Belief in Partnership

By "belief in partnership," we mean the conviction that senior stars are owners of the firm, and that regardless of the legal form of ownership, it must be governed as a partnership. As described in chapter 6, this

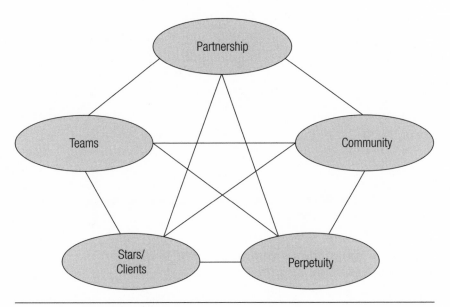

Figure 7-2   The Cultural Core

means consensus building among the partners before major decisions about strategy are taken and the involvement of senior stars in other aspects of the governance of the firm, such as how compensation is allocated and who is advanced into the ranks of the partnership. It also means that although it is all right for senior stars to compete with one another, it is *not* all right to let these rivalries get out of hand. The firm's success is the result of the efforts of the group as a whole. Respect for one another as colleagues is critical despite the fact that on an immediate, Monday-morning level, on any given day, one senior star may be pulling ahead of another in compensation, or in client portfolio size, or on another front altogether.

Diamond Cluster has been a public company since 1997. Nevertheless, the officers of the company still refer to, and think of one another as, "partners" and approve each other's compensation. If there were serious dissent about the compensation, the partners could remove the CEO and other senior managers. Similarly, the partners vote on new additions to their number. All of them feel that Diamond is their firm, and the leadership and management responsibility is spread among them, even though much of the equity is publicly owned. Mike Mikolajczyk, one of the firm's vice chairmen, explained their approach this way: "The partnership feeling is maintained through certain processes, like nomination. Every partner gets one vote, regardless of seniority or equity stake. So even the youngest junior partners feel like real partners and an important part of the process." An important corollary to these convictions, he noted, is the belief that "as owners, we are financially interdependent and must work hard for the firm's success."

A small event at Goldman Sachs, which took place at a leadership seminar in the early 1980s, says volumes about that firm's belief in partnership. A seminar for a group of Goldman Sachs partners was held just days after the firm had incurred a significant loss in its fixed-income trading activity. By coincidence, none of the partners from that part of the firm were in attendance. At the time, it was the custom to kick off these sessions with a talk and a question and answer session with the senior partner, John Weinberg. After some brief comments, the first question Weinberg was asked concerned the loss. Before he could answer, other partners expressed their concerns; implicit in their comments were criticisms of the fixed-income partners responsible for the loss.

Weinberg's response? If the firm was going to make as much money as it did on the upside, the partnership also had to expect some losses. He went on to confide that those involved had come to him personally—some of them practically in tears—and that nobody felt worse about what had happened than they did.

Implied in Weinberg's words—very thinly veiled—was the partnership mindset: Don't go around casting blame on your partners, who have already accepted their responsibility. The right thing to do is to support them. Just as you'll be supported if you encounter a rough patch.

Partnership, in the legal sense, was the founding form of many PSFs, and this belief takes its roots from that fact. The Goldman Sachs example we just mentioned took place long before the firm went public. But make no mistake; the partnership *mindset*—the core belief in a sense of shared destiny—is very real in all of these firms, regardless of ownership structure. The events described above, with a different cast of characters, could happen at Goldman today.

Belief in Extraordinary Teams

In all the firms we studied, the work of serving clients is performed by constantly changing teams of professionals. Because the need to serve clients well and in a timely fashion is paramount, life in those teams can be hectic and complicated. There's always a temptation for team members to want to look good and advance their own careers to the detriment of their teammates. This core belief discourages that kind of behavior. It also sends a strong signal about how you should relate to the people with whom you work every day on project teams: people with whom you may very well be competing for advancement or income, and under circumstances in which the tradeoffs between getting credit for yourself or for the team may be acute and personal.

This belief mitigates the tension among stars as they strive for personal success while simultaneously serving clients well together. (In that way, it is a natural extension of the belief in partnership that guides the senior-most stars of a firm.) Young stars learn that they must work together to succeed. Being an effective team member is what counts; that's how you succeed personally. In the words of Pat Gross, founder and chairman of the executive committee at American Management Systems:

> I think part of our advantage is the way we put effective teams together. If you deconstructed our teams and looked at the individuals, I'm not sure we could argue that the individuals by themselves are substantially better than other people. But there is a very strong, team-oriented culture at AMS. We say, "Let's get the right people together to solve a problem," and there's a lot of bonding that goes on. We have a common mission: the project team. It's the body of the company. When people come in, that's what they see. That's what they hear. When they come, they join a project team, and if they're not comfortable with that, they don't stay around very long. People try to communicate this in the recruiting process, because it's at the core of the way people at AMS think and operate.

Belief in Community

Belief in community is the proposition that at the end of the day we're all part of one firm, and we are expected to work together and help each other. A natural extension of the two beliefs that precede it, this one is all-encompassing and includes everyone, not just partners or senior stars, no matter the location. People in the United States, people overseas, people in every practice area (remember the example with which we started the chapter). This belief keeps everyone working together, regardless of specialty, level of experience, or geographic location. It keeps in check the tension that naturally develops as people identify with the goals of their particular part of the firm.

"People can't be worried about who gets the credit, and they can't be worried 'this is my deal, my client, stay out,'" said one Goldman

Sachs banker, talking about the day-to-day efforts of the firm. "In order to serve clients, we need to bring together the skills related to hundreds of products and we have to bring to bear many parts of the firm. There needs to be a culture of excellent communication and commitment to the idea that if the firm does well, we will all do well, as opposed to 'I need to figure out how to look good, how I can do better.'"

As Patrick Pittard, CEO of Heidrick & Struggles, put it, "If you're in a ditch, you've got people who are there with you trying to get you out. You're not alone in troubled times. Say you have a search that has gone all the way through the process and you think you have it completed and then at the last minute the candidate bails out on you. Well, you send a voice mail and you get thirty responses on how to help yourself."

Belief in Stars First/Clients First

We've been arguing, up to this point, that the people you pay are more important than the people who pay you. We've been emphasizing that point because we recognize that the natural tendency is to put clients first, and we wanted to stress the strategic importance of stars. But the fact is, in these outstanding firms, stars and clients are considered equally important, and a natural and constant tension exists as each sector vies for the center position on the firm's radar. You can't have satisfied clients without stars, and you also can't have stars without satisfied clients.

The dilemma truly is that straightforward. If you're overinvesting in your clients, you'll lose your stars. But if you don't meet clients' needs because of your stars' desires, you won't be competitive. The belief that both are equally important enables firm managers to work for a balance in meeting conflicting demands between clients and stars. Diamond Cluster deals with the importance of both constituencies in an interesting way: Young professionals at Diamond are told "Clients first, firm second, yourself third." Partners, however, are told that the emphasis should be "Stars first, clients second, firm third." Whether stars or clients are given priority at any given time depends on circumstances. But over the long run, the balance between the two is critical to success. If the firm is to succeed, therefore, both these constituencies must be proactively managed, and each must think ultimately it occupies the number one spot.

Belief in Perpetuity

This core belief refers to the shared understanding, at the senior level, that you and your peers are building a firm that will transcend generations. That you're not only "in this together" with your current fellow partners, but also that part of your job is to help create a firm that will endure so future partners can succeed. It's the long view, and it drives people to behave selflessly in ways that support the firm.

Like many other New York law firms, Skadden Arps was challenged by the economic downturn in the late 1980s. The firm had always maintained a performance-based compensation scheme tied to each partner's contribution to firm results. But in the worsening economic climate, Joe Flom, one of the senior partners, along with several peers, became worried that the younger generation of partners would earn so little that the firm might lose many of them. Their proposed solution? That the older partners take a cut in pay so that the next generation could be better compensated. The partners approved the plan. And the result was not just a change in the partner compensation plan but also a reaffirmation that the firm was built to endure, that each generation should worry about the next.

What happens when questions arise about how to distribute the wealth among different generations at your firm? How do clients get passed on from retiring partners to their younger peers? This belief in perpetuity guides those kinds of events—balancing the tensions between older and younger stars and achieving results that work for the long-term success of the firm.

Culture and Consequences

In aggregate, these core beliefs constitute a way of thinking about how an individual star fits into the ecosystem of a firm. The beliefs shape how people behave on Monday morning, but they do not *specify* that behavior in an absolute sense. The belief in partnership, for example, motivates senior stars to collaborate as partners; the details of that collaboration change as the partnership expands and diversifies. Just as a belief in *democracy* or *capitalism* propels governments and markets, so do core beliefs propel outstanding PSFs.

The interdependence of these core beliefs is striking. In the absence of one or more beliefs, a firm will eventually stumble. Without "partnership," a firm will gradually disintegrate at the top, as senior stars compete among themselves. Without "extraordinary teams," clients will be underserved and promising young stars will resign for more fulfilling employment opportunities. Without "community," an organization of independent silos will rapidly evolve—a place where knowledge is hoarded, resources are never shared, and quality inevitably deteriorates. If a culture is unable to balance stars and clients, sooner or later one will win at the expense of the other (and either stars or clients will defect). Finally, without a belief in perpetuity, a firm will, at a minimum, *underinvest* in the future—and more than likely sell out to the highest bidder whenever an attractive cash-out opportunity presents itself—without considering whether this is in the long-term interest of the firm's owners.

There is no escaping the direct linkage between culture and consequences. In robust economic times, commercial success may mask cultural deterioration. In downturns, the flaws become readily apparent. As the Japanese say, "A falling tide exposes all rocks." Culturally strong firms accommodate and adapt to recessions, while culturally flawed firms struggle to hold ground. Culture can emerge as the defining competitive advantage, in part because it is impossible to copy. Individuals in great firms rally around a powerful cultural core, while in other firms, they obsess over their personal circumstances as their business flounders.

Consider Goldman Sachs, whose business principles reflect the firm's commitment to its core beliefs. Written down many years ago by John Whitehead, then one of the managing partners, they are still published in the annual report each year (see box 7-1). The message is clear to employees and to clients. Regular publication is one small way that Goldman nurtures commitment to these core beliefs.

Box 7-1 Goldman Sachs's Business Principles

1. Our clients' interests always come first. Our experience shows that if we serve our clients well, our own success will follow.

2. Our assets are our people, capital, and reputation. If any of these is ever diminished, the last is the most difficult to restore. We are dedicated to complying fully with the letter and spirit of the laws, rules, and ethical principles that govern us. Our continued success depends upon unswerving adherence to this standard.

3. We take great pride in the professional quality of our work. We have an uncompromising determination to achieve excellence in everything we undertake. Though we may be involved in a wide variety and heavy volume of activity, we would, if it came to a choice, rather be best than biggest.

4. We stress creativity and imagination in everything we do. While recognizing that the old way may still be the best way, we constantly strive to find a better solution to a client's problems. We pride ourselves on having pioneered many of the practices and techniques that have become standard in the industry.

5. We make an unusual effort to identify and recruit the very best person for every job. Although our activities are measured in billions of dollars, we select our people one by one. In a service business, we know that without the best people, we cannot be the best firm.

6. We offer our people the opportunity to move ahead more rapidly than is possible at most other places. We have yet to find the limits to the responsibility that our best people are able to assume. Advancement depends solely on ability, performance, and contribution to the firm's success, without regard to race, color, religion, sex, age, national origin, disability, sexual orientation, or any other impermissible criterion of circumstances.

7. We stress teamwork in everything we do. While individual creativity is always encouraged, we have found that team effort often produces the best results. We have no room for those who put their personal interests ahead of the interests of the firm and its clients.

8. The dedication of our people to the firm and the intense effort they give their jobs are greater than one finds in most other organizations. We think that this is an important part of our success.

9. Our profits are a key to our success. They replenish our capital and attract and keep our best people. It is our practice to share our profits generously with all who helped create them. Profitability is crucial to our future.

10. We consider our size an asset that we try to preserve. We want to be big enough to undertake the largest project that any of our clients could contemplate, yet small enough to maintain the loyalty, the intimacy, and the esprit de corps that we will treasure and that contribute greatly to our success.

11. We constantly strive to anticipate the rapidly changing needs of our clients and to develop new services to meet those needs. We know that the world of finance will not stand still and that complacency can lead to extinction.

12. We regularly receive confidential information as part of our normal client relationships. To breach a confidence or to use confidential information improperly or carelessly would be unthinkable.

13. Our business is highly competitive, and we aggressively seek to expand our client relationships. However, we must always be fair competitors and must never denigrate other firms.

14. Integrity and honesty are at the heart of our business. We expect our people to maintain high ethical standards in everything they do, both in their work for the firm and in their personal lives.

Culture Binds

Goldman Sachs's decision to go public might provide the best example of a case where culture—including the firm's core beliefs—sustained the firm through a time of incredible change.

For over ten years, under the leadership of three capable individuals, Steve Friedman, Jon Corzine, and Hank Paulson, the partners of Goldman Sachs debated the merits of selling some of the firm's equity into the public market. The partners had decided to take on two limited partners, the Bishop Estate and Sumitomo Bank, to raise needed capital in 1986, 1992, and 1994 without abandoning the partnership form of ownership. But the discussions about becoming a corporation and selling equity to the public continued throughout the 1990s. At least six times, the partners vetted the issues thoroughly, declining to go public for the last time in 1996.

In 1998, the discussions again gained momentum, culminating with a Quaker-style meeting of all 190 partners at a location outside New York City at which the partners aired their hopes and concerns about the proposed public offering. "For people who have devoted their lives to this place, it was exhausting, but in some ways amazing," one partner told the *New York Times*. "People did not hold back."[1]

The arguments for selling 15 percent of the firm's equity to the public were mainly financial. It was a means to realize the immense value of the firm's equity for its partners and to raise capital for the firm's future.

Most apropos to the topic of culture were the reasons put forth for not going public. The fear was that the core belief in the partnership, as we have called it, would be lost, endangering the firm's ability to serve clients and attract stars. At the final meeting, partner after partner, even those in favor of the idea, voiced this concern.

Finally the partners voted for the IPO, in essence authorizing the firm's management committee to work out the offering terms and timing.

The IPO isn't the end of the tale, however. The firm sold 15 percent of its equity to the public (and subsequently made a secondary offering of 40 million shares) and Goldman Sachs is legally a corporation, but the senior leaders and the partners have done all they can to retain a partnership culture. The firm retains the partner compensation plan for which up-and-coming stars are chosen, just as before they were elected into the partnership. The firm retains a partnership committee as one way of giving voice to its partners. Meetings of the partners are still held to discuss important issues and decisions. In the eyes of the public and the capital markets, Goldman Sachs may be a legal corporation, but in the eyes of its senior stars it is culturally still a partnership, and they are working to sustain this culture.

Convictions, which people hold dear, are not easy to alter. So when a decision that might affect "the way we do things" comes to bear, it's only natural that a partnership—and an organization at large—would be reluctant to make the move. Recognizing that a strong culture is like glue can help you overcome such concerns. Culture binds organization, strategy, and stars together in the face of significant requirements for change. It can help retain core beliefs and values while allowing major changes in strategy or organization.

So when a firm goes from private to public, as Goldman Sachs, Korn/Ferry, and so many others have done, the firm's leaders can use the cultural beliefs associated with the partnership to maintain the alignment that would otherwise be threatened. The formal trappings associated with public shareholders—quarterly earnings reports, a board of directors, for example—can be handled in a manner that supports rather than threatens beliefs about partnership and community.

The same holds true for international expansion where a firm's culture can provide a blueprint for foreign offices. As McKinsey expanded globally to eighty offices in thirty-two countries, replicating the culture was a critical imperative. Despite immense variations in nationalities and time zones, professionals share a common set of beliefs about partnership, teams, community, and clients and stars.

Culture is a stronger force for unity and coherence than any formal document could ever be because the stars of a firm with a strong culture have an emotional commitment to their beliefs. The Goldmans and McKinseys of the world have been able to maintain consistent strategic and organizational approaches due to the strength of their cultures. Wherever these firms operate—from New York to London to Delhi to Tokyo—their professionals share a culture that binds them into common practices, sustains their alignment, and gives them an advantage in attracting clients. Clients perceive a clear and consistent strategic identity because the firm's professionals—wherever they work—share a set of beliefs that maintain this consistency.

This is especially true when firms are experiencing rapid growth. Growth delivers a double whammy; it exacerbates organizational complexity and introduces legions of "culturally raw" recruits. Both characteristics may easily undermine or confuse cultural beliefs. When a firm hires partners from industry or completes an acquisition, the dynamics are even more challenging. Yet firms with strong cultural beliefs are bound together despite these centrifugal forces. Weaker cultures on the other hand are blown asunder. This in part explains why mergers and acquisitions of PSFs so often fail in retaining stars. The culture of the acquirer overwhelms the culture of the acquired, and this alienates the stars of the acquired firm, causing them to leave.

Strong cultures bind together organizations during times of strategic change—ranging from IPOs to international expansion to acquisitions. Once again, core cultural beliefs help sustain competitive advantage for established firms. How might this apply to first-generation PSFs?

Culture Builds

First-generation professional firms always struggle and most do not succeed; building an enduring firm is exceptionally challenging. Nowhere was this more evident than in Internet-focused technology consulting, a sector that experienced a spectacular run-up and an equally spectacular fall. Although few of these companies will survive, much can be learned from the role that culture played in their rapid growth and subsequent collapse.

In 1996, Bob Gett, founder and CEO of newly formed Viant, began to create his organization's culture from scratch. After a lengthy professional career, at firms ranging from Fidelity Software Development Company to Cambridge Technology Partners, he well understood the importance of culture. In fact, to emphasize the power of culture, he dubbed himself the "Chief Cultural Officer." While Viant's culture was a critical ingredient in its ramp up to over $150 million revenue in four years, it was even more important as the industry collapsed and Viant saw its market capitalization decline by 95 percent.

Viant's belief in partnership was forged as Gett recruited his senior team. Strong capabilities were necessary but not sufficient to get in on the ground floor of this "new economy" consulting firm. "I looked for culture builders who shared a dream about Viant's potential," explained Gett. These values and beliefs became the common denominator across what was otherwise a diverse leadership team.

The top ten leaders (they were never referred to as "managers" or "executives") met for a day to write down their shared beliefs as a touchstone for the expanding organization. Even before they specified the full details of their business plan, these "partners" shook hands on their cultural contract. Their desks were arranged together in the large open space that was the firm's new office. "We were desk to desk every day," said Gett. "There was no escaping our shared beliefs as leaders in this venture."

The cultural belief in extraordinary teams was integral to Viant's competitive strategy. Traditionally, clients had purchased business strategy services, creative services, and technology assistance from different firms. Viant intended to change this paradigm, to blend the three disciplines from very different worlds, to innovate at the seams where the three intersect. To better serve clients, Viant needed to somehow operationally integrate the strategic skills of a Bain & Company with Ogilvy & Mather's creative talent and IBM Consulting's technology capabilities—and to do this effectively on every single client team!

Part of the solution resided in performance management. Teams (rather than individuals) were held jointly accountable for projects. Consistent salary ranges and performance criteria were applied regardless of a consultant's expertise. Peer review became an integral component of annual performance reviews, which subsequently determined bonuses and career progression.

Performance management systems reinforced the cultural belief in diverse but integrated teams. As the firm grew, the culture shaped and informed behavior, encouraging opinionated consultants to be compassionate about each other's views. The belief in extraordinary teams (and a potential competitive advantage) was born.

Viant's core beliefs in partnership and teams provided the foundation for a pervasive belief in community. This was not some "feel good" factor to add a dose of "cool" to the business mix. On the contrary, this cultural dimension was carefully designed to help deliver on the company's strategic ambitions.

"People here are really pounding away," explained Gett during the firm's heyday. "They have to feel great about sitting next to other guys and gals in the room." Thus the rationale for an office layout that contributed to spontaneous interactions. "Vianteers," as Gett called them, also abhorred hierarchy. It took four years before the community generated its first organizational chart.

Office size was capped at 125 people to avoid diluting the sense of community. New offices were "spawned" by permanent and temporary transfers to new locations where their primary job was to inoculate the emerging communities with Viant's cultural beliefs.

A belief in community was not only critical to retain and motivate stars in an exceptionally competitive space; it was absolutely necessary to facilitate effective knowledge sharing. Gett believed that typical consulting firms deliver client value that rests primarily on the strength of an individual team, rather than on the knowledge and energy of an entire firm. Gett intended to harness the "power of the community" to develop a culture of knowledge sharing and learning, a place where "silos" and consulting "rock stars" gave way to selfless collaboration. In 2000, *Fortune* profiled Viant in an article entitled "The House That Knowledge Built."[2] It referenced community-building tactics ranging from a three-week new-employee orientation (called "Quick Start"), to staffing rotations that created networks of personal relationships across the firm. While these systems reinforced a sense of community, it was the cultural belief that dictated daily knowledge sharing across organizational boundaries.

The community orientation was deliberately designed to provide excellence in servicing clients. How, then, did such a client-centered culture trade off between its star performers and its important clients? As Gett explained: "We always take the high road in balancing the demands of our clients against the needs of our consultants, even though we may suffer short-term pain as a consequence. The high road means that we never compromise the client situation, that we primarily take their view. Our cultural belief is that people will be taken care of, that their sacrifices will be recognized."

Trading off in favor of current clients did not mean sacrificing the future of the firm, however. In a powerful cultural statement, Viant management decided to constrain their growth during the 1998/1999 halcyon days of market expansion. "We were concerned that excessive growth would undermine our culture and potentially create client excellence problems," said Gett. Despite competitive pressures to maximize growth, spiced by media commentary that Viant was falling behind, Viant held growth to a modest 100 percent per year (compared to the 300 to 400 percent typical for the industry at the time). "We wanted a culture centered on being the best, not the biggest, to strive for mind share rather than market share," Gett proclaimed.

This perspective and the values it reveals were central to Gett's dream of Viant's endurance. "Viant was not 'built to flip' like so many venture capital–funded start-ups," he told us. "I have always been driven by commitment to people and excellence, rather than ego or money. Hopefully, Viant will be 'built to last.'"

At this time, the jury is still out on his ambition. The bursting bubble of e-commerce has led to profit shortfalls, layoffs, and consolidation throughout Viant's industry. Once again, however, Viant's cultural beliefs have come to its aid—though probably not enough to save it. Because the firm nurtured a belief in perpetuity early on, employees were better able to view the market turmoil from a long-term perspective. The intense pain of layoffs was tempered by the understanding that it was "the right thing to do for the firm." "Survivors" were motivated to fight the good fight and do whatever it took to survive and prosper. Voluntary turnover has remained at a low (by industry standards) 12 percent despite the harsh reality that employee equity is virtually destroyed.

Whatever the future holds in store for Viant, the value created by its culture is unmistakeable.

Culture Bends

A strong culture is a common attribute of successful professional firms. Most of the leaders of the outstanding firms we've

interviewed, in fact, believe that culture is one of their key competitive advantages. McKinsey's legendary leader, Marvin Bower, for
example, consistently emphasized the importance of being a "true
professional" regardless of circumstance. That cultural attribute is still
central to the firm because it is a large part of what makes McKinsey,
McKinsey. It is a critical piece of the firm's strategic identity and a
strong draw for clients.

But if culture can be a competitive advantage, it can also be a
competitive disadvantage. What if a fast-paced, aggressively informal
e-commerce consultancy is pitching to a traditional, conservative, industrial company? What if that consulting firm—whose livelihood depends on a client base that includes such traditional companies—is
unable to present its case in a way that resonates with the manufac-
turer's executives? If your culture is working against the firm, you
have to change it. You start from where you are—what lies ahead is
up to you.

Consider how dramatically the culture at Ogilvy & Mather
changed under the leadership of Charlotte Beers. When Beers took
over as CEO and chairman of Ogilvy & Mather Worldwide in 1992,
the firm was losing important clients and facing declining revenues.
The agency had just been acquired in a hostile takeover by British holding company WPP, and morale was low. Star performers knew that
their game plan wasn't working, but they were suspicious of Beers, of
Sir Martin Sorrel, WPP's CEO, who had chosen her, and of change
under Beers's rule. Sorrel, they feared, was focused only on the bottom
line, and wasn't interested in preserving the dedication to creative values in which they deeply believed—values instilled by the firm's legendary founder David Ogilvy. Beers, for her part, was also personally
suspect because, as she put it, she was "the daughter of a Texas cow-
boy," whose past success had not been with a big international Madison
Avenue agency, but rather with a smaller, domestic firm in Chicago.

Put another way, the stars at Ogilvy were worried that Sorrel and
Beers represented great threats to the firm's founding culture—a culture they were proud of and part of—a culture that had once made the
firm a great success.

Beers understood that, and what she did showed the firm's stars that not only did she acknowledge and respect Ogilvy's culture of creativity but she also knew what to do to build on that foundation, instill new, critical core beliefs, and return the firm to greatness in its new context.

In her first few months at Ogilvy, Beers spent a lot of time talking with investors and clients. She knew that the culture at Ogilvy was something to be preserved and strengthened, but she also came to the realization that the firm had no clear direction. By May 1992, she had mustered a group of Ogilvy employees—some heads of key offices or regions, some creatives, some account directors—who she felt were on her wavelength. These were people who wanted to sustain the culture but also understood the need to reinvent the agency's focus and structure. This "thirsty for change" group, as it was called, met first in May 1992 in Vienna, essentially to raise issues, to talk about what it would take to reinvent and revitalize the firm. Among their primary concerns was Ogilvy's geographic fragmentation—the firm was run essentially as a group of national kingdoms and was not set up to meet the increasing global needs of multinational clients in a seamless way. Basically, the firm's culture lacked a core belief in community.

They met next in August 1992 at the English resort Chewton Glen. Out of that meeting came the "Chewton Glen Declaration," which set three strategic goals for 1993: (1) client security—focusing energy on current clients; (2) Better Work, More Often—a call to move beyond the traditional Ogilvy credo, "We Sell, Or Else," and develop ways to make brand the binding focus of the firm; and (3) Financial Discipline—a call to get control over the firm's resources. Mostly, the goals were a call to reinforce the firm's values about creativity, but in a way that better met client needs.

Shortly thereafter, Beers made a major change in the firm's structure. She created a third dimension in its matrix organization: World-wide Client Service. (The other two are geographic and functional.) The purpose of the new dimension was to put a capable leader, Kelly O'Dea, in charge of encouraging cooperation and coordination in serving global clients across the high national barriers that were part of the old culture. When the agency won the IBM worldwide account, the need for the change became evident to everyone in the firm; without the new structure—and the corresponding new belief in the "global community" philosophy—Ogilvy could never have provided seamless service to such a multinational client.

Reduced to its essentials, the old culture just didn't work as well as it needed to in a changing marketplace. Beers and her "thirsty for change" friends used their leadership skills, their new ideas about the importance of brand, and their new structure to support the important embedded beliefs about creativity and tie them more closely to the brand needs of clients. At the same time, they enhanced the core belief about the importance of community.[3]

So What?

Each generation transmits its culture to the next. In older firms, that means that the culture has been passed through many generations, often through stories—some accurate, others probably myths. What matters isn't absolute veracity but rather that the intended message gets through.

Remember the partners at Goldman Sachs, for example, who say they received their first performance review from former senior partner Gus Levy while they were in the men's room with him. True? Well. . . . But even if the accounts aren't entirely accurate, they're amusing, they get attention, and the message is clear: "We believe in performance reviews and they're going to be direct and personal."

Figures like Goldman Sachs's Levy, McKinsey's Bower, Ogilvy & Mather's David Ogilvy, and Fulbright & Jaworski's Leon Jaworski become somewhat larger than life through such oral histories. But beware. It's too easy to think of culture as something personal—the stuff of legends and heroes. In fact, the notion that culture flows from any few leaders—no matter what their stature—is true mostly in a figurative sense. No single leader can embody the culture of any given firm, especially if that firm has hundreds, or thousands, or tens of thousands of employees. Most of the members of the firm never see the top brass.

And if they do, it's for a few minutes each year, when they are on a stage or appearing in a videotape.

A firm's culture will be influenced to a modest extent by the sheer force of personality coming from the person on that stage. What they say and how they say it does have an impact. But, as we've said, culture is influenced more substantively through the decisions that a person— and "partners" throughout the firm—make, which then shape behaviors, which subsequently become part of "how things are done here."

In other words, if you're the leader of your firm, you may be the walking personification of the culture you inherited when you took office. And that may be a good thing. But your firm's culture isn't set in stone. It isn't ever "done." The way that you will affect it most is through the strategic and organizational choices you make or facilitate every Monday morning.

In PSFs, these choices are particularly challenging, because firm leaders lack the positional power and authority of their peers in traditional corporations. In the next chapter we will explore what it means to lead without control, especially at the most senior level.

8 ★ Leadership without Control

The Power to Persuade

P EN IN *hand, he sat in his study, his journal
turned to a blank page. At last he began
writing:*

*Tomorrow my life will change. For years I've dreamed of
leading an organization, shaping its future. Now my partners—
at least the majority of them—want me to run the firm. I'm
sorry Mike P. announced his resignation. But just because he
brings in big clients doesn't mean he can manage a complex organization like ours.*

*Am I ready? Yes! There's no job description for the manag-
ing partner—just do whatever it takes to build a profitable,*

enduring firm. In the short term there's no question that means generating more revenue. Our numbers are down, although there seem to be pockets of strength in certain places and practices. Who knows? Then there are those nagging questions about new markets and new competitors. And the organization: I know I need to make a bunch of changes to fix the structure and that will mean replacing a number of the partners currently in key leadership roles.

In the end, I guess it's all about people. How do I get buy-in to the changes? To my/our decisions? How do I actually get my partners to do *what I want them to do—especially when so many of them have their own agendas and don't really know (or trust) me? We don't have the luxury of leisurely debate—the marketplace won't wait.*

I can't do all this alone. Somehow I've got to get consensus and keep the firm moving in the right direction without igniting turf battles or provoking turnover we don't want. We've got to put the firm first, but everyone's naturally obsessed with their own circumstances. How am I going to get all the individual pieces of this crazy puzzle aligned, even for a while?

No matter what, I have to stay true to my values and beliefs. Do what's right for the long-term interests of the firm and our clients. Not let myself get overwhelmed by the immediate pressures.

And what about me? I'm excited, but I haven't even begun the job and already I feel like a magnet for everyone's problems; crap is coming at me from all directions. No one who hasn't been here can understand what this is like. The responsibilities seem endless. What will I be remembered for years from now? And how do I survive in the meantime?

I'll figure it all out . . . somehow.

It's a basic management precept: Design an organization so that its managers have authority commensurate with their responsibility. The theory is to avoid holding leaders accountable for things over which they don't have control, and in principle, it's nice, neat, and wise. In reality, organizations are rarely this orderly. Leaders are often asked to take responsibility for activities over which they lack direct control. Nowhere is this more evident than in professional service firms.

In PSFs, many people occupy formal leadership roles. These range from practice leaders, to office managers, to chairs of firmwide governance committees. They include partners accountable for recruiting, knowledge management, professional development, and marketing. With the common exception of the CEO, most of these professionals reduce (but don't eliminate) their client responsibilities. They are producing managers, responsible to the CEO and ultimately their partners for delivering results. Unlike their peers in traditional corporate structures, however, they lack the positional power to enforce their decisions—even at the chief executive level.

Chief executives lead PSFs like boxers with one hand tied behind their backs. Although they are held—and hold themselves—personally accountable for firm success, they lack the authority vested in a typical corporate chieftain. Sometimes their titles reflect these constraints: They are "managing partners," "senior partners," or "managing directors." Regardless of their titles, rarely in business does effective leadership demand such skill and finesse while yielding such enduring benefits to an organization.

Leadership is critical to a firm's success precisely because of the inherent characteristics of the PSF business model. Without strong leadership, the necessary diffusion of power throughout a firm can paralyze decision making and undermine alignment. If leadership is too forceful, however, partners will reject its imposition on their autonomy. The result must be a delicate balance of power between a firm's leaders and the partners they serve. In this chapter, we will focus on the role of the senior leader, the firm's CEO. Our perspective is relevant, however, for anyone who holds—or aspires to—a leadership position in a professional service firm. (See figure 8-1.)

Limits to Leadership

Being the chief executive of any company is a demanding job. Carrying out the responsibilities of a CEO in a professional service

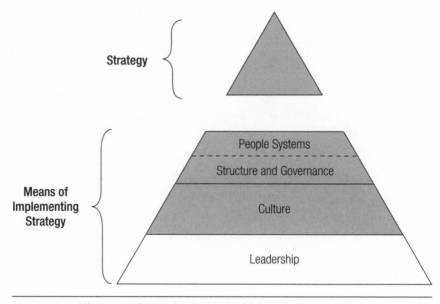

Figure 8-1   Alignment Pyramid: Leadership

firm is exceptionally challenging because the position lacks the inherent power and control that CEOs of traditional companies enjoy. We've made this point before. But we want to review the key differences briefly from the perspective of the CEO because the implications are crucial: for how the job of the senior leader is defined, and for what successful performance in the job requires.

The differences begin at the beginning. In conventional corporations, the CEO is selected by a higher authority (the board of directors) acting on behalf of the shareholders, which gives him strong positional power to shape the company's direction, strategically and organizationally. The PSF leader starts with a different hand of cards. Regardless of the specific mechanics, he is chosen directly or indirectly by the very people he is expected to lead. In addition, his peers also have an ownership interest in the firm. So unlike the senior executives in a corporation, who defer to their bosses' judgment, these senior stars believe they have the right to question, debate, and even oppose initiatives with which they disagree—and often do so.

Corporate CEOs also tend to deal with their shareholders periodically and at a distance. True, they have to talk with analysts at least quarterly, and they may receive inquiries from concerned shareholders. But this is a far cry from the PSF CEO, who lives and works among her "shareholders." She passes them in the hall, eats lunch with them, and has to guide them productively to accomplish her objectives. Even if they work in distant locations, partners are never more than an e-mail or a telephone call away. When they have any concerns or suggestions, the CEO will hear them in real time. Professional service firm leaders are always in the midst of their partners and fellow owners, which is one reason we use the phrase "leading from within."

Finally, there's the important matter of who decides the CEO's tenure. In traditional companies, if the board of directors believes the CEO is doing a fine job, he stays until he reaches retirement age. If the directors think otherwise, sooner or later he leaves. In PSFs, the situation is strikingly different. The CEO serves at the pleasure of the partner-owners. Many firms require that he be reelected and/or restrict the number of terms he can serve. Even in firms that have public shareholders or corporate parents, removing the firm leader can only be done effectively with the consent of the senior stars. If the stars don't like the idea, the consequences for the CEO's successor and the shareholders can be an unproductive and distracted organization, in which professionals who go down in the elevator one evening may not return the next morning.

Together, these dynamics ensure that the CEO's role in the professional service firm's decision making is both constrained and complex. Suppose a corporate CEO believes his company should make an acquisition or embark on a major European expansion, for example. While any competent CEO would discuss the initiative with his direct reports and, one hopes, gain their support, most subordinates will read the tea leaves and endorse their boss's thinking unless they believe he is way off base. They are, after all, employees not partners; the decision and accountability ultimately accrue to the chief executive. As for the board of directors, only a stream of wrong decisions is likely to stir its concern. In contrast, in a PSF, the CEO can't undertake a new strategic initiative without the buy-in of the senior stars who will have to lead and fund the effort. Trying to force support through arm-twisting is a sure recipe for failure, as we saw in chapter 3. The only effective course of action is to facilitate a consensus among the partners that the new direction is sound.

Similar constraints apply to organizational choices. Suppose the issue is a decision to promote a successful young person to lead a significant business unit. A corporate CEO will typically solicit input from others, including the vice president of human resources. Essentially, though, it's the CEO's call, and the executive who's being asked to take the new assignment will likely feel immense pressure to accept. (Although candidates can turn down formal leadership opportunities, most realize that doing so is apt to be what's often called a career-limiting move.)

In a PSF, the process is more opaque. True, the managing partner usually can select whomever she wants to assume leadership responsibilities as an office head, say, or a practice area leader. It's part of the CEO's job. Getting her colleague to accept the position is a different matter, however. An outstanding attorney doesn't want to sacrifice her clients to manage an office. An executive search professional refuses the headaches associated with leading a practice area. Information technology consultants resist management assignments, for fear they'll become "administrators." Aggressive investment bankers prefer doing deals to managing people. Accomplished advertising stars prefer the creative process to management hassles. Expert accountants prefer accounting. Often the response to an opportunity to assume a leadership position is "Thanks, but no thanks!"

What leverage does the managing partner have? Not a lot. While a conventional CEO can offer a compensation increase, or talk about subsequent career opportunities, or even threaten dire consequences if the offer isn't accepted, the PSF managing partner has no such ammunition. His partner's compensation is largely determined by the firm's partner-compensation agreement and by the firm's and his personal performance. Besides, the compensation committee would have to approve any unusual change for the person in question. A promise of increased management responsibility is unlikely to be a major carrot. Finally, of course, there's no way the managing partner can threaten to drum his colleague out of the partnership if he doesn't accept.

Comparable limits circumscribe other organizational choices. If the CEO wants to add a new management position, he has to convince his colleagues. If he thinks a change in the firm's measurement system—or even worse the compensation scheme—would improve alignment, it means more discussions with the senior stars and maybe the creation of a committee to study the issue and come up with a recommendation to all the partners. If the question is one of bringing a lateral hire into the partnership, or even which young stars to promote, the CEO cannot make the decision alone. At a minimum, he has to develop an informal agreement among his senior colleagues. Often the firm's governance process dictates that the decision be made by all the partners (or a subset of the partnership) whom the CEO can influence but not control.

The Subtle Art of Building Consensus

Given this environment, it's not surprising that CEOs of successful PSFs are masters of building consensus and facilitating decisions so that the key players will agree with and support them. At any point in time, the CEO may be shepherding dozens of discussions and decision cycles, each with its own process, set of participants, and timing. If he is realistic, he plans each process as carefully as possible—then goes with the flow depending on the reactions and resistance of his partners.

Every decision confronts different obstacles and moves ahead at a different pace. Some decisions are abandoned. Others take unsuspected twists and turns. The leader's job is to ensure that critical decisions are made thoughtfully and in a timely fashion—even if the ultimate choice is different from his own. Marvin Bower, the leader who shaped McKinsey in the 1950s and 1960s, engaged in discussions with his colleagues over many months about whether the firm should change its legal form from a partnership to a corporation. Bower opposed the change, while the majority of his partners supported it. Bower was persistent and pursued this discussion with his characteristic energy, until he realized that most of the partners had a different view about what would be in McKinsey's best future interest. In the end, the firm became a private corporation, as it remains today.[1]

On matters where the CEO has a legitimate voice, the best CEOs are proactive and open in their efforts. When Rajat Gupta created a committee of up-and-coming partners to spark a dialogue about McKinsey's long-term strategy, his partners rightly saw the initiative as his responsibility. Similarly, the partners at Goldman Sachs found it altogether appropriate for three of the firm's CEOs to initiate discussions about whether to become a corporation and sell stock. When the partners finally did decide to go public, after almost a decade of deliberations, the strong consensus to go forward reflected the work done by three generations of leadership.

When the decisions relate to matters (such as compensation and promotion) that clearly belong to the partners, however, the CEO must be more circumspect. As we saw in chapter 6, PSFs often create ad hoc committees and initiatives to deal with specific issues in addition to their standing governance committees. Moreover, in many of these firms, some of the committees (or at least a few of the members) are elected by the partners, so that the committee will act as a check-and-balance on an overzealous chief executive.

This creates a delicate situation for the CEO. He wants to make sure the compensation scheme or promotion process is working smoothly and that the partnership is reaching the right decisions. But he does not want to appear to be interfering in matters that are officially none of his business. Successful leaders negotiate this situation by keeping their antennae tuned and listening to committee chairs and members to understand what is happening. In these conversations, they can also react and express their own opinions. In a healthy firm, it would be rare for a committee or its chair not to take the opinions of the firm's leader into account. But skillful leaders approach these discussions with tact and a recognition that the final decision must rest with the committee and the partnership.

None of this is quick—or easy. Anyone who has tried to bring together colleagues with diverse points of view will recognize that getting them to agree is not a simple undertaking, especially when they are the people who put you in your job as well as your co-owners.

Seeking agreement and building consensus is even more difficult when a firm is confronting serious challenges, as many are today. While an inexperienced reader might think that building consensus is simply a matter of rational logic backed up by persuasive rhetoric, nothing could be further from the truth. However "small" the issue, there is usually a great deal of emotion and irrational logic involved. That is why bringing about a meeting of the minds requires a healthy dose on the leader's part of what psychologist Daniel Goleman calls "emotional intelligence."[2]

Among the components of emotional intelligence, three are particularly relevant for anyone engaged in building consensus. The first is *self-awareness*, the ability to understand your own moods, emotions, and motivations. "Why am I reacting as I am?" "How is my internal state affecting my capacity to assess others and their points of view realistically?" Being self-aware allows a leader to clear out the emotional underbrush and gain a clear perspective on what colleagues are feeling.

Next is *self-regulation*, the ability to keep your emotions in check, to suspend judgment, and to think before acting. When trying to forge an agreement among several partners, the worst thing you can do is lose your cool. You need to control your own emotions and responses to move the discussion toward an agreement rather than into an increasingly angry debate.

The third is *empathy*, the ability to put yourself in another person's shoes and understand positions that differ from your own. Empathy allows a leader to understand and respond to someone else's emotional reaction without letting his own emotions get in the way. In a sense, PSF leadership is like being a professional tennis player: In both cases you're most likely to prevail if you can keep your own emotions in check.

Claiming that every professional who held a leadership position in the firms we studied had a high level of emotional intelligence would be a gross exaggeration, but describing the CEOs of these firms as long on emotional intelligence is a safe bet. Implicitly, these attributes were among the things that had made them attractive to their partners when it was time to select a new CEO.

The Leader's Job

In the annals of leadership, no image is more familiar than the dynamic individual inspiring the masses from behind a podium. In the corporate version, the CEO's insight and vision energize his audience of managers and employees, motivating them toward greatness. The business prospers; the chief executive is a hero.

While this scenario may be possible in some circumstances, it's a nonstarter in PSFs. It conflicts with the inherent business model, with the governance constraints within which the firm's leaders must work, and with the requirements for long-term firm success. As we've seen, PSFs are built day by day, year by year. They are rarely the products of a single bold stroke or an act of inspiration. Even major strategic initiatives like acquisitions quickly evolve into long marches. Leadership in this context has a lot more to do with the details of managing a complex organizational and economic system effectively than it does with delivering the occasional inspiring speech.

When chief executives are selected, they take responsibility for their firm's future performance and for the well-being of everyone connected to it: owners, employees, and clients. The leaders we interviewed consider this responsibility as a kind of sacred trust, believing that it is their job to ensure that the firm not only achieves its goals but also effectively pursues the activities necessary to reach those goals. The duties that will fulfill this mandate are rarely codified in formal job descriptions or long-term plans, however. Instead each CEO must define his own particular set of activities, which will both reflect the firm's culture and norms and signal the initiatives he thinks necessary to ensure the firm's future, given its competitive environment and the needs of its current and future stars.

A firm's initiatives are defined by and shape its strategy. The chief executive functions, therefore, as the firm's strategic champion: refining strategic goals, facilitating strategic decisions, and ultimately implementing a wide array of operational imperatives that support new initiatives. While no single individual can define a firm's direction alone, the CEO must be the ultimate custodian of this effort.

This responsibility translates directly into how and when re-sources, in the form of both people and cash, are allocated. A firm's strategy, whether addressing today's problems or tomorrow's opportu-nities, is manifest in its resource deployment across geographies, business lines, clients, and initiatives. Every investment involves com-plicated tradeoffs: Even in the largest firms, pursuing one mix of activ-ities necessarily constrains other possibilities. Accomplished CEOs work constantly within their management and governance systems to direct resources here or there, so that they will be allocated consis-tently with its strategic needs.

So what do leaders in PSFs *do?* How do they approach the onslaught of Monday morning, replete with its myriad problems and opportunities? While the specifics vary, depending on each firm's particular circumstances, several practices characterize the best lead-ers in the best firms. These practices remain consistent year after year, and they are supported, in one way or another, by how these leaders allocate their time, constitute their staffs, and design their in-formation systems.

Understanding Reality

Opinions are interesting; facts are critical. Successful leaders obsess over understanding the reality of their business circumstances. They avoid the tendency to become inwardly focused. Instead, they continu-ally assess the dynamics at their firm's strategic perimeter. They monitor aggressive competitors and track their firm's win/loss ratio across geog-raphies and business lines, for both clients and recruits. They carefully examine innovations, be they new concepts, technologies, or service strategies. Whenever possible, they collect data about their strategic identity, the marketplace, and their firm's relative position in it.

Internally, leaders design feedback loops to augment this external data. This feedback comes in many forms: firmwide employee surveys, office surveys, project team debriefings, upward feedback, skip-level interviews, 360-degree feedback, and exit interviews. The tactics vary, but the goal is the same: to understand reality in a practical manner that helps them guide the business and make the right choices about how to allocate firm resources.

Financial metrics can clarify reality or mask it. Often, financial reporting systems are designed more for auditors than general managers. Successful leaders customize their systems to generate useful data, especially surrounding product line profitability. Despite the complexities of a matrix structure, they insist on understanding as clearly as possible exactly where the firm is making and losing money. The *where* might include geographic locations, business lines, product or service types, customer segments, or even groups of partners. Some firms go so far as to determine profitability by individual partner. The motivation is consistent: Understanding how and where a firm makes money is a precursor to making more of it.

Perhaps the most important way that CEOs understand reality is by listening. One chief executive refers to himself as the "Chief Listening Officer." If you followed outstanding CEOs around for a year and transcribed every conversation, you'd likely discover that effective CEOs listen at least twice as much as they speak—and the speaking time would include a lot of questions. They listen to clients and potential clients, partners and recruits. They engage in dozens of simultaneous conversations via e-mail, phone, fax, and memo. They are directly connected to the field, to their firm's strategic perimeter, to the partners, clients, staff, and recruits who are their constituents.

Like many of these leaders, Ed Meyer, CEO of Grey Advertising, travels around the globe several times a year to test and refresh his understanding of his organization's problems and opportunities. In conversations with key leaders, he probes to learn what they think the future holds and how they feel about the firm. Such travels enable a CEO to listen to the firm's stars and share her ideas about possible means to solve pressing problems or seize opportunities. CEOs aren't just note takers. They have points to make and themes to reinforce, which they do in every imaginable setting from one-on-one conversations to formal speeches. They also understand that effective communication is about receiving as well as broadcasting: understanding and appreciating the perspectives of stars, who want to be heard and resent sermons. As a result, CEOs emerge from their travels and conversations with a sense of the issues and where various colleagues stand on them. They better understand reality and can better anticipate what lies ahead.

The further and more accurately a leader can see into the future, the better. Like the driver of a rapidly moving car, if the CEO can focus on the edge of the headlights, the firm is more likely to travel safely through the changing environment. Suppose you were the CEO of a major accounting firm in the late 1990s. What would you be thinking about? Quite possibly, what—and when—the SEC will finally decide about allowing accounting firms to do consulting work; or whether and how you might expand into legal services. Or put yourself in the shoes of the managing partner of a large, successful law firm: What's on his strategic perimeter? Issues like, will the big accounting firms get into the legal profession? How will the growing number of law firm mergers affect us? Should we consider an acquisition or a merger? What about expanding outside the U.S.?

When chief executives perceive new challenges, they take the responsibility to get the discussion going and accelerate the dialogue. They bring facts to bear in order to help others appreciate the reality of the firm's circumstances. They confront the issues, acting as truth tellers. In doing this, they further develop personal perspectives about what's really important and how best to proceed. While they rarely mandate decisions, they have their own sense of direction and argue for it. By prompting debate, they are able to better understand reality and influence the behavior of their stars.

Developing and Guiding Stars

Outstanding chief executives are outstanding starmakers. Attracting, developing, and motivating a diverse group of highly competent professionals is their most prominent competency. These CEOs, as we've seen, are both bosses and peers, and their span of control (the number of "subordinates" who report to them) is decidedly limited. Broader—and far more important—is their span of influence, which is defined by their personal relationships with stars throughout the firm. Most, but not all, of these stars are likely to be partner-level professionals, while another contingent will be made up of younger stars with leadership potential. To varying degrees, these stars act as the CEO's emissaries and sounding boards. They form the group around which the CEO facilitates key decisions. (Because they are dispersed among business units, functional groups, and offices around the world, they also provide a reality-check for the CEO's understanding of the state of the firm.)

A broad span of influence is particularly critical in a large firm, where a CEO cannot possibly influence everyone directly. The chief executive must work the organization through intermediaries and avoid the detachment imposed by a narrow span of control. The span of influence becomes his vehicle for nurturing loyalty—to the firm, its strategic goals, its values, and its leadership. This loyalty, in turn, reinforces his ability to orchestrate key decisions.

A few key decisions matter a lot in shaping star behavior. The most leveraged are leadership assignments, promotions, and budgets (or financial controls). Putting the "right" people in the "right" jobs is central to effective leadership; a CEO, as best as possible, must pick her team. Promotions, especially to partner, provide another opportunity to influence the firm's future. The same is true of budgeting decisions and financial management.

Although PSF leaders cannot allocate resources nearly as freely or absolutely as their corporate peers, they consistently use budgeting and planning processes as an avenue to build consensus around the firm's resource priorities. They lobby and cajole other firm leaders to help shift resources from one area to another. They pressure individual partners to take on new assignments, supporting major initiatives. They place people who endorse their resource agendas in pivotal management roles. And as best as possible, they track actual resource allocations—people, time, and cash—to evaluate progress against their goals.

None of these decisions are as powerful in influencing stars' behavior and building loyalty, however, as rewards. Rewards begin—but do not end—with partner compensation. Compensation practices, as we discussed in chapters 4 and 5, have an enormous impact on the motivation of individual stars and the firm's overall culture and values. For this reason, the CEO needs to be sure that the firm's financial incentives are encouraging the appropriate mix of behavior. That its compensation scheme is perceived to reward actual results (both individual and firmwide). That people feel their compensation is fair, in relation to their role and relative to what peers are paid within the firm and outside it.

Because significant compensation decisions are vested in others as part of the firm's governance apparatus, the CEO's participation is always a balancing act. On the one hand, he has to ensure that the compensation system is reinforcing the appropriate behavior among stars and promoting overall alignment. On the other, he cannot appear to be sidestepping firm governance, where it is officially none of his business. Consequently, he walks a fine line and also employs nonfinancial rewards to further influence stars.

The power of nonfinancial rewards in influencing professionals can't be overestimated. We have seen senior stars jump through hoops (literally!) to receive a Lucite block trophy at a partner meeting. Astute chief executives bestow recognition in all its wonderful forms: personal attention, public accolades, special internal assignments, extra vacation, client opportunities, speaking opportunities, media interviews, awards, gifts, offices, first-class travel, technology allowances, season tickets, and important-sounding titles—to mention only a few!

Stars, always competitive, love to be distinguished from their colleagues in as many ways as possible. While compensation is motivating, it is generally private and not something you can point to throughout the year. (Chances are, people are thinking more about *this* year's compensation than last year's in any case.) When did you last see a pay stub hanging proudly on someone's office wall? On the other hand, we've all seen tombstones (deals done), photographs (celebrities known), awards (personal achievement), client mementos (value added), framed articles (public recognition), books published (intellectual contributions), and technology gadgets (systems installed) adorning offices.

An effective CEO shapes star behavior and nurtures loyalty through a myriad of recognition tactics, some as simple as acknowledging birthdays, some as complex as formal promotions. He also employs these and other methods to build a continued supply of future leaders within the firm.

Leadership Supply

Nothing is forever, least of all a leader's tenure. In a PSF, part-time leaders rotate on and off governance committees, and in and out of important management roles. Even chief executives often have term limits—explicitly or implicitly. To further complicate the situation, professionals are recruited and often promoted on the strength of their professional accomplishments, not their leadership skills. Professional service firms are typically short of skilled leaders, especially when they're growing. Turnover makes matters worse. So successful CEOs worry a lot about ensuring an adequate supply of leaders, well suited to the future needs of the firm. They accomplish this through thoughtful planning, leadership recruiting, and career development.

Most firms underestimate their need for future leaders. They fail to appreciate fully the compounding effects of firm growth, leadership turnover, and career life cycles on the supply and demand of leaders. The challenges of filling leadership positions from the outside (remember "fit"?) cause most firms to grow leadership talent from within. If they fail to do so, they have little recourse except to place mediocre leaders in positions of authority—or slow their growth. But lacking the fundamental characteristics and skills necessary to succeed, mediocre leaders cause problems, sooner or later. They may fail amidst a blaze of partner dissension or, worse yet, manage to hang on to power while stars abandon the firm and the organization deteriorates. Weak leadership is to a PSF what a toxic spill is to an underground aquifer: Unnoticed at first, it contaminates the organization from within, silently polluting it until its quality is lost.

Successful, enduring firms understand this risk, as do their chief executives. These CEOs continually analyze their leadership supply and demand, planning at least five years in advance. (Leaders are not created overnight, and the long cycle time often traps unsuspecting firms into developing too-few capable leaders.) They identify and recruit future leaders both into the firm and from the ranks of successful practicing professionals. They know the qualities they seek and use the firm's performance management systems (such as rankings and reviews) to help identify candidates. They rely heavily on the judgment of their best lieutenants (qualified leaders themselves) to choose the next generation. In sum, the process is not left to chance. It is as explicit and deliberate as the budgeting process (although usually not as visible).

A generous supply of potential leaders encourages a firm to invest in leadership development. On-the-job learning and personal mentoring are by far the most effective tactics. As we saw in chapter 4, people learn more by doing than by sitting in a classroom engaged in a week of formal training sessions. Special assignments, job rotations, and even office transfers all fuel a potential leader's on-the-job learning. As relevant experience accumulates, mentors (themselves experienced leaders) further coach and assess the firm's future leaders.

Coaching is an act of dialogue: about issues that need attention, about how to persuade a star to take on added client work, about what to say to a partner who is having difficulties with a client. In smaller firms, these dialogues can take place during every walk down the hall. In larger firms, they may unfold in a weekly or even daily telephone call. In either case, the dialogue is constant—and two-way. The CEO is acting as a mentor and advisor, but he is also learning about his younger colleagues and the challenges they face.

Perhaps the most significant leadership development issue every CEO faces is who should be his successor. This is the ultimate governance question facing any firm's partners, and like other governance issues, this matter often belongs to the partners. Typically, it is none of a sitting CEO's business. Yet ignoring the matter may be a disservice to his partners and to the firm. Effective CEOs understand that leaving the emergence of a capable successor to chance can be a risky course. They also recognize that exercising too heavy a hand in the decision may offend their colleagues, disrupt the process, and tarnish their legacy.

The solution to this conundrum is to focus consciously on the development of the next generation of potential chief executives. Partners want a choice. Even if one person emerges as the obvious answer, the fact that there are other viable candidates is important. For the partners, it provides calibration and reduces dependency. For the new leader, it provides legitimacy: Her predecessor hasn't foisted her on the firm. The CEO will "end high" by putting the firm first.

All this represents a significant investment: Leadership development can consume a substantial amount of senior stars' time, and there are no guaranteed outcomes. Wise CEOs accept the cost because they appreciate the negative consequences of a leadership shortage. At the same time, they understand the difference between investment and speculation and place their bets accordingly. They know that their chosen candidates will need to have a high level of professional competence. But they also know that all the technical skill and expertise in the world won't help if their candidates lack the personal characteristics essential for leadership success.

The Fundamentals of Leadership

When you observe outstanding chief executives across professions, as we did, what's noticeable is what you *don't* see. They are neither the smartest, nor the most successful, nor the most experienced in their firm. What characterize these men and women is *who* they are as human beings. Colleagues of these CEOs use various terms to describe their characteristics. We think the three words that capture them best are *character*, *judgment*, and *intuition*.

Character

In PSFs, leaders exercise influence more than they do control. How does a CEO influence others to support a strategic initiative, or assume new responsibilities, or accept a personally unpopular decision? *Character*. A leader may be articulate, relentless, and superbly competent, but that's not enough. People won't respond to her influence unless they not only respect her professional capabilities but also trust her as a person.

Trust is the bedrock of influence. People who trust one another don't second-guess one another. They communicate honestly and fully because they are confident of each other's motives and intentions. Colleagues believe in their integrity, knowing that they are focused on the best interests of the firm and that they will "do the right thing." Absent trust and respect, a leader's influence deteriorates. People won't let themselves be persuaded by someone they don't trust. They may smile and say the right things, but they won't follow the leader. This is a natural and rational reaction because it's risky to follow someone whose values and beliefs you don't respect.

The most outstanding CEOs we know share a few deeply held beliefs, which shape their behavior day by day:

- They believe that their firm is more important than any single individual, including themselves.

- They believe that the leader's job is to help others succeed.

- They believe in their firm's future; their horizon extends beyond today to encompass subsequent generations of partners and clients.

If you think back to the five core beliefs that characterize great and lasting firms (which we discussed in chapter 7), you'll see immediately why these CEOs are superlative culture carriers. Their beliefs are consistent with their firms' defining principles. They can walk the talk because the firm's values and their personal values are reinforcing.

They can also walk the talk because they possess the personal characteristics that are essential to lead successfully from within. They are confidently humble: They can present a strong point of view without being egotistical or acting superior. They have bandwidth, the flexibility and maturity to address a wide array of human issues, even if they don't necessarily like all the people involved. They take personal accountability for events and actions that are outside their direct control—and accept the related consequences. They give credit rather than taking it (or, as the University of Alabama's famous football coach "Bear" Bryant is reported to have said, "The victories belong to the team, the losses are all mine"). Last but hardly least, they have the empathy and understanding that build bridges of loyalty throughout an organization.[3]

These values and related behaviors are not about sainthood; they're about survival. A leader who lacks this kind of character will eventually fail in the demanding context of a professional service firm. Professionals who lack such character aren't promising candidates to fill management positions, let alone become the next CEO.

Judgment

A person's character, who she truly is as a human being and how she sees herself in relation to others, defines her potential for influence. Her judgment determines how well she will realize her potential. The world is filled with smart people of admirable character who lack judgment. These people inevitably make poor decisions in both their personal and professional lives. They also make poor leaders.

The second fundamental characteristic of successful leaders is sound judgment: the ability to make thoughtful decisions across the thousands upon thousands of issues that confront a general manager. How do I best motivate this partner or reprimand that one? Whom do I promote? Whom do I place in which critical jobs? How do I communicate, to whom, when, about what topics? When do I participate in which decisions? When do I confront a problem, and when do I look away? How do I spend my time? The list, of course, goes on and on. Most decisions are incremental and tactical. As a result, the quality of a chief executive's judgment is largely hidden from view— until the consequences begin to play themselves out. The cumulative effect of poor judgment can erode a firm's intangible assets and undermine its potential.

Intuition

If a person in a leadership position has a flawed character or chronically poor judgment, he will fail—it's only a matter of when. Conversely, solid character and sound judgment will produce success, which intuition will magnify.

There are many types of intuition ranging from an eye for talent to a nose for new business. All of these are useful; however, the intuition we're especially concerned with relates to manipulating complex organizational systems. The best PSF chief executives have an uncanny ability to understand all the moving parts of their business, and how these parts directly and indirectly influence one another. Like a master chess player, they anticipate cause and effect many moves ahead. For instance, they foresee the second- and third-order consequences of placing a certain partner in charge of an office: how that decision might prompt other aspiring office managers in other locations to react, and the downstream implications of those reactions.

Understanding the myriad organizational networks that compose PSFs is another hallmark of this intuitive systems thinking. Professionals participate in many informal networks defined by the firm's structure (practice groups, for instance, or geographic clusters). More subtle networks create linkages among partner generations and personal friendships. Recognizing and accommodating these multilayered connections helps PSF leaders anticipate unintended consequences and therefore make decisions that will reinforce the firms' alignment.

An individual's intuition is as fundamental as his judgment and character. All three attributes are more or less established by the time a person reaches adulthood. Together, they constitute a basic profile that determines someone's leadership capability. Training, coaching, and incentives may influence behavior, but they won't alter a person's fundamental characteristics. Like it or not, we are who we are.

Managing Alignment

The importance of alignment in creating and sustaining a successful firm has been a recurrent theme throughout this book. In previous chapters, we examined the strategic choices, organizational decisions, and cultural factors that determine whether a firm is more—or less—aligned. Now it's time to look at the last piece of the puzzle: the part the firm's senior leader plays in bringing about alignment.

If anyone is in the position to be alignment's architect, it is the CEO. He is the person at the center of the strategic and organizational decisions that move a firm into (or out of) alignment. It is the CEO's job to develop a broad perspective across all the firm's practices and offices, a personal knowledge of many of its professionals and all of its stars, and a sense of the firm's future needs and the choices that will be required to address them. So while he may not know all the details of his firm's far-flung activities or all its personnel, he does have a sense of the whole. That, in turn, is essential in addressing the complex and constantly evolving design problem that alignment represents.

Managing alignment is usually a process of continual fine-tuning rather than a series of periodic blunt thrusts. The chief executive is always pushing here and pulling there, modifying this policy or changing that person's responsibilities. Barring a major change in the firm's circumstances, managing alignment is an incremental process, much like the work of trimming the sails in a yacht race. America's Cup victories are won by tiny artful adjustments to a powerfully designed vessel. So it is with aligning a firm.

Because change is accelerating in the markets in which PSFs compete, alignment is best thought of as a moving target. The challenges the Internet consulting firms faced when the value of their stocks plunged provide a dramatic example. (The loss of luster in their strategic identity; the fall in the value of the stock options, which were a key part of their compensation plans; the necessity to lay off talent—all these knocked their alignment into a cocked hat.) But the sources of strain on a firm's alignment can come from anywhere, including its own initiatives.

Recall Charlotte Beers's addition of the Worldwide Client Service dimension to Ogilvy & Mather's structure. The decision met well the need to create an integrated effort, across functions and among the firm's far-flung offices, in support of global clients like IBM. But the new structure was inconsistent with the existing compensation system, which was tied to country and functional outcomes. Because many of the local offices had minority owners whose rewards were contractually tied to country results, this scheme couldn't be altered quickly. The consequence: confusion and frustration for Beers, until the compensation system could be redesigned to fit the new structure and strategy, and the firm once again became more aligned.[4]

Few firm leaders have the concept of alignment explicitly in mind when they make strategic and organizational choices. Mostly, they are focused on immediate cause-and-effect relationships: If we ask this person to move to the London office, we can give that person more responsibility and room to grow. When they do think about alignment explicitly, they tend to view it as an end in itself rather than as a dynamic process: If we change the compensation scheme to reward business development more highly, we'll get stars who are more focused on finding new clients.

In contrast, the best PSF leaders grasp the systemic nature of alignment. This is what Charlotte Beers understood: the need to keep her firm's strategic and organizational choices as mutually reinforcing as possible, so that it sent an integrated set of signals to its stars about what they needed to do and how they needed to behave to achieve their goals. Leaders like Beers recognize that there are complex connections, both direct and indirect, among the choices they make to shape the firm's strategy and organization. They don't have to wait until they hit a bump in the road—in the form of unintended consequences—to realize that they're working with a system in which everything connects.

Ted Mirvis, a member of the management committee at Wachtell, Lipton, Rosen & Katz is a leader who understands these complicated connections very well. Here's how he described what could happen if his firm's lockstep approach to compensation (in which all the partners in the same generation get the same pay) were to be changed:

> Suppose you decided to keep everything else the same, but eliminate lockstep. What would happen? Look at what happens at other firms. People would feel huge pressure. Someone would say, "Well, then, basically I'm only going to get paid for what I generate. And I'm really good at bringing in a certain kind of business, but that kind of business requires a large associate base. So I need to have a pool of ten associates." Change one thing, and immediately, there would be pressure to change other things. And there would be a change in the environment as well. You'd hear things like "You can't

tell me not to do that. I need to do that to bring in business. If you're going to tell me I can't bring in more associates, then I'm going to get paid less at the end of the year. What gives you the right to tell me I can't?"

Not many people are as articulate as Ted Mirvis about the complex web of relationships that ultimately produce alignment. And as we said earlier, this kind of systems thinking can be hard to grasp. For people whose minds do work this way, however, a little consciousness-raising can be a very useful thing. That is why one of this book's goals is to help more leaders explicitly identify (and factor into their decision making) the complex system that fundamentally defines their firm and its culture.

How Do You Know If You're Succeeding?

In PSFs, the chief executive is the one individual whose full-time job is to guide the firm toward its future goals. For this reason, the only effective way to judge the CEO's success is to evaluate the state of the firm and, in particular, the degree to which it is an aligned and profitable business, well positioned to win in tomorrow's marketplace. Carrying out such an evaluation involves looking backward, at past achievements, while simultaneously looking forward at future potential.

Lagging Indicators

A natural inclination when evaluating a leader's accomplishments is to look backward, to examine the firm's financial performance. (This is especially true when a firm's profits are rapidly rising or falling.) If done rigorously, this look in the rear-view mirror will identify important trends indicating success . . . or the lack thereof. Sophisticated firms measure financial performance across a number of variables: revenue growth, price realization, utilization, operating margins, profit per professional and cash flow per partner. By applying these metrics to business units and/or practice areas, firms can identify the underlying financial dynamics driving their business—and provide a basis from which to extrapolate future performance.

A second rear-view image is the popularity of the CEO among his partners. Since the chief executive essentially works for his colleagues, popularity is of more than passing interest. In some firms it will dictate whether a leader is reelected. Partners' perceptions may not accurately reflect reality, however, since their opinions are strongly influenced by the nature of their personal relationship with the CEO, the financial performance of the firm, and their personal financial rewards.

Rich partners, not surprisingly, are happy partners. During prosperous times with big year-end bonuses, partners may tolerate wide variations in the quality of their leadership. When profits (and partner compensation) decline, however, the pressure on the CEO to provide solutions increases dramatically. Therein lies the danger of judging leadership success by historic financial figures and popularity alone.

In any given year, a firm's financial performance depends on initiatives and decisions made in prior years. In other words, this year's profits are in reality a return on last year's assets, or even the last decade's assets! Why? It requires at least five to ten years to develop a star partner. Profitable large-scale client relationships are the product of years, not months. Strategic identity is the result of thousands of diverse experiences. Professional service firm assets are built cumulatively, as we've said, person by person, client by client, day by day.

While assets are painstakingly slow to build, they can be demolished rather quickly. If a CEO, under pressure from her partners to "make the numbers," desires, she can encourage any number of decisions that are likely to prop up short-term financial performance at the expense of long-term asset building. This tradeoff can easily become a contract with the devil, setting off a downward spiral whose full consequences may not become apparent for some time.

How does this happen? Leaders fire professionals in an effort to cut cost, which demotivates the surviving stars so much (and violates the cultural norms) that turnover escalates, causing previously loyal clients to defect. Recruiting costs are slashed, dramatically constraining the future pool of stars and shrinking the potential supply of firm leaders. Projects are pitched and sold outside the firm's areas of expertise just to bolster revenue—an approach that dilutes its strategic identity and siphons off scarce resources to unproductive activities. Knowledge generation and training budgets go unfunded, further diluting the firm's ability to add value. Promotions are delayed, causing stars to defect to competitors. The list goes on and on. Some of these tactics may be wise, others foolhardy. But in all cases, they mortgage tomorrow's assets for today's returns.

In judging leadership success, therefore, you cannot simply analyze lagging indicators. It is imperative to look as far ahead as possible, examining the *leading* indicators that more appropriately define the future value of a firm.

Leading Indicators

As the ultimate day-to-day custodian of his firm's future, the CEO's foremost responsibility is to enhance the firm's intangible balance sheet and improve its competitive position. While the future is always uncertain, two sets of leading indicators allow you to at least anticipate future performance.

The first set is strategic. To what extent has the firm made progress against its strategic goals? How is it performing in the marketplace, against its direct competitors, in serving its target clients? What is the depth of its cumulative knowledge and experience supporting each line of business, and how has that evolved relative to competitors? What is the level of penetration in the most important geographic markets? What is the cost and quality of the firm's services, relative to competitors? Is there any sign of strategic obsolescence or strategic drift? Are past strategic decisions proving to be thoughtful moves on a multidimensional chessboard, or costly (even disastrous) shortcuts?

Assessing a firm's strategic performance must be customized to the firm's specific circumstances. What's critical, however, is that the firm look outside itself, asking tough questions about its true competitive performance and avoiding the natural tendency to focus exclusively inward.

The second set of leading indicators tracks the intangible assets that drive the firm's business model. Not surprisingly, those assets begin with the firm's stars.

Stars. As we've stressed repeatedly, stars drive a firm's success. Evaluating this talent pool, especially its size and quality, is central to judging leadership success. This assessment is both relative to the past (for example, is the firm more or less star rich than it was five years ago?) and to the marketplace (for example, is our star capability stronger or weaker than our direct competitors?).

The loyalty of stars to the firm is one critical attribute of these intangible assets. Is it headed in the right—or wrong—direction? What is the level of star turnover? Are stars more or less motivated than they were one year ago? How long do they expect to remain with the firm?

Another critical attribute is the knowledge the firm's stars generate and apply. With the notable exception of research firms, clients don't buy knowledge per se. They buy what knowledge can do for them—that is, the knowledge the firm's stars apply. Effective knowledge management systems are inputs to a firm's client value proposition and may improve its quality, service, and productivity. Knowledge in the form of intellectual property may further differentiate a firm, although such differentiation is typically short-lived, as we saw in chapter 3. Knowledge enables firms to compete. Stars and their capabilities, bolstered by knowledge, determine the effectiveness of that competition.

Recruiting is the lifeblood of a PSF and central to growing its supply of stars. Is the firm attracting star recruits? What is its performance in recruiting versus direct competitors? How is the firm perceived within the markets (such as graduate schools) from which it sources talent?

While most PSFs are chronically short of the talented leaders required to fill their management positions, from CEO on down, such shortages can be both problematic and costly, as we've discussed. Not surprisingly, therefore, the firm's ability to replicate its success in subsequent generations is another criteria against which to evaluate its CEO's performance.

Clients. The strength of a firm's client assets depends on the propensity of its current and past customers to purchase its services in the future. Getting repeat business means overcoming two challenges: "Does the customer have needs consistent with the firm's capabilities," and "Is the customer loyal?" It is tempting, but wrong, to extrapolate from past experience in addressing these issues. In a dynamic marketplace, past sales do not predict future revenue—just ask the "new economy" Web consultants!

Client assets can be evaluated by understanding client retention, client profitability, and the underlying dynamics of customer loyalty.[5] What is the firm's share of a client's total business? Why do clients remain active, and why do they defect? When competing for business, whom does the firm lose to, and why? What is the status of client assets across geographies or within practice areas? What is the flow of requests for proposals, in quantity and quality? Is the overall client portfolio stronger or weaker than it was three years ago? These questions cannot be answered definitively, but they lend themselves well to data collection and analysis.

External Strategic Identity. In chapter 3, we highlighted the many constituents with firsthand experience of a firm: from recruits to alumni, from clients who selected you to those who didn't. The experience of this disparate group of individuals gives them credibility with other less-knowledgeable individuals. Collectively, they become the firm's representatives, who may or may not encourage the phone to ring with new business opportunities. They have a point of view, often adamant, about your firm's relative strengths and weaknesses. Their composite view becomes the firm's external strategic identity, its core brand value in the marketplace. Advertising, business development, and outreach may augment strategic identity and enhance awareness among target customers. But in a world where clients' perspectives remain heavily influenced by word of mouth, a firm's external strategic identity drives its revenues—for better or worse.

Organizational Assets. The last set of intangible assets relates to alignment. Organizational assets are the means by which a firm's strategy is implemented. Organizational choices (people systems, structure, and governance) and leadership combine with culture to create (or undermine) a firm's alignment. Organizational assets reflect alignment in action: Does the organization function overall in a way that drives the firm toward its strategic goals? Or, far more common, is all or part of the organization broken, producing a two steps forward, one step back (or even three steps back) scenario?

Organizations are highly dynamic and imperfect things; they are always flawed in one way or another. Yet firms with a wealth of organizational assets are easy to spot if you know what to look for. For instance: decisions, once made, are followed through on. People systems are aligned with cultural norms, and both reinforce the firm's competitive differentiation. The processes that guide decision making function well; partners are satisfied with both their level of participation and the direction of the firm.

Organizational assets can be judged by the participants involved in the organization. Do the key leaders and senior partners feel the organization is well aligned? On balance, does the organization encourage stars to act in the best interests of the firm, or not? Do the various elements of the organization seem to fit together, or are there glaring inconsistencies? Periodically surveying partners (on an anonymous basis) can shed light on the answers to these and related questions.

Judging leadership success is not simple. It requires transcending a historic perspective to identify and track leading indicators across both strategic and asset-related dimensions. The breadth and complexity of these variables reflect the challenges of leading a professional service firm in the twenty-first century. In addition to these challenges, CEOs must add one more: managing themselves. This is not a matter of life goals and tradeoffs, or long-term career planning (which we discuss in chapter 9). Rather, it refers to the specific issue of how a professional can survive and flourish in a leadership position.

Surviving Leadership

Professionals without formal leadership responsibilities may have difficulty appreciating the daily demands confronting their leaders. Responsibility without enough control, limited hierarchy, and a complex business model combine to generate enormous stress, especially for the chief executive. Stars demand attention on today's problems, while the leader is simultaneously attempting to address tomorrow's opportunities. A broad span of influence requires time to build and maintain numerous personal relationships. The leader is accessible to her many constituents, and consequently vulnerable to being inundated by points of view, demands, and distractions. We've observed how PSF chief executives manage themselves through these pressures. There are no magic answers, and every individual's circumstances are different. That said, a few basic principles seem consistent—principles that transfer directly into a leader's daily behavior. Combined, they outline a set of best practices.

1. *Prioritization:* Successful leaders ruthlessly judge which issues can be ignored, for now (or even forever), and which require disproportionate time.

2. *Acting Ahead:* In any given year, a significant amount of effort is devoted to next year's challenges (or even the year after). Leaders avoid the trap of overinvesting in today and thus failing to build for tomorrow.

3. *Personal Pacing:* Leaders control themselves and don't overreact. They understand that professional service firms may feel fast paced, but in reality change occurs quite slowly.

4. *Devouring Feedback:* Leaders are peers, yet different. People don't tell them everything they need to know about their performance. Some will emphasize only what they think a leader wants to hear. Accomplished leaders aggressively solicit personal feedback from all reliable sources, lest they find themselves disconnected and ineffective.

5. *Learning:* Leaders pursue learning voraciously. Previous professional experiences cannot fully prepare people for these roles. They find advisors and coaches, within the firm and outside it.

6. *Recharging:* The demands of leadership drain personal batteries, which can rapidly undermine performance. Enduring leaders recharge themselves weekly in whatever manner best suits them, from concentrated family time to exercise to entertainment. When times are really tough, there's an understandable tendency to skip recharging—when, of course, one needs it the most.

7. *Being a Player/Coach:* Even full-time leaders stay connected to clients. It's fun, enhances their credibility with their partners, and keeps them informed.

8. *Addressing One's "Use By" Date:* No leadership position is—or should be—forever. The best leaders plan ahead for their own transition and succession. They understand that if they don't take control of this, others will eventually do so for them. Many leaders have a natural tendency to hang on too long, rather than pass the baton to the next generation. Others leave with their firms in good shape, which is the best way to be remembered.

We've said that CEOs have challenging jobs, but so do all partner-level executives in PSFs. It is not too much of an exaggeration to say that the firm becomes your life. It occupies almost all your waking hours and, perhaps, your dreams as well. Is this any way to live? Is it good for you? Is it good for the firm? How do you build a successful future career, whether you're thirty or fifty? These are the issues to which we turn in our final chapter.

9 ★ Aligning Your Star

Build a Life, Not a Resume

JENNIFER WAS *struggling. She and her younger colleague, Mac, were already well into the main course and uncorking a second bottle of wine, but she seemed to be getting nowhere. Mac's questions were thoughtful and unrelenting.*

"Sure, I'm on the fast track at our firm, but where exactly is that taking me? As a new partner, I expect to make sacrifices and work hard. And I certainly appreciate the big bonuses. But is this really what I should want for the rest of my life? I'd like to keep growing professionally, keep on developing my skills. And over time I want to be able to make some tradeoffs—to invest in my family, my community, and my personal passions. How

will more years in the firm help me accomplish those goals?
You're an ambitious person with a broad array of interests and
commitments, Jennifer. Don't you ever feel this way? Why are
you still here?"

   In fact, despite the two decades that separated them, Jen-
nifer had often asked herself the same questions over the years.
At this very moment, she was wrestling with whether to retire
early from the firm and pursue a leadership role with the local
community foundation. The headhunter had been persistent—
and Jennifer was genuinely intrigued.

   The dinner ended, and Mac and Jennifer went their sepa-
rate ways. They were mentor and mentee, colleague and friend,
exploring similar questions.

   Eighteen months later the office celebrated as Mac landed
the biggest account of his career. He e-mailed Jennifer at the
community foundation to share the great news.

This scenario (with variations) is played out daily in professional firms. Personal aspirations collide with firm realities; conflicts rage among a person's competing interests. Stars are inherently ambitious and restless, creating a certain amount of unavoidable turmoil for themselves and their colleagues.

   If that turmoil transfers into lower productivity or, worse yet, star turnover, a firm can find itself in deep trouble. As we've said all along, the destiny of the individual and the firm is not easily separated when the underlying business model is powered by professionals (see figure 9-1). Stars sell and serve clients. Stars lead and follow the firm. Their skills, motivation, and behaviors determine the firm's ultimate success or failure.

   Thus we now turn the spotlight on you, our readers—the professionals who *are* these organizations. More specifically, we look at why—and how—the concept of alignment can be as powerful on a personal level as it is when applied to the direction of a firm overall. This is critical for your business, as well as for yourself.

   As you've seen, alignment is created when a firm's strategy, organizational choices, culture, and leadership are mutually reinforcing. In practice, this means that alignment is always a cumulative conse-

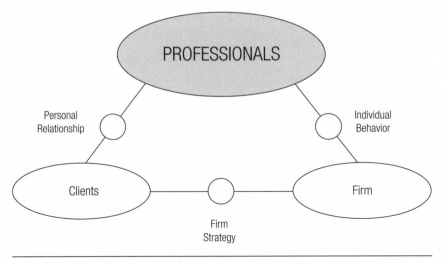

Figure 9-1 **PSF Business Model: Powered by People**

quence of hundreds of separate decisions and thousands of individual behaviors. "Aligning the stars," the metaphor we've used to capture this phenomenon, suggests that alignment can propel a firm toward its strategic goals and lead to financial and competitive success.

The process of aligning your own star unfolds in a similar way. Like an organization, an individual's decisions and behavior can be aligned with his or her own capabilities, goals, needs, and values or not. Such personal alignment is hard to calibrate on any given day. But its presence (or absence) almost always becomes apparent over time, as life unfolds. Contrast the people you're familiar with who seem to lead happy and fulfilling, though not necessarily easy, lives with those who seem perpetually discontented, whatever their achievements, and you will recognize the phenomenon. The former have achieved personal alignment; the latter likely have not.

Every life is shaped to some extent by circumstances: a lucky break or a fortunate decision. You heard about a job opening from a friend. You received a great job offer at a prestigious firm because you were "on" in the interview. You bumped into your future spouse (of forty years) at a wedding that you almost decided not to attend. Things happen to us that drive our destinies in unforeseen ways. More fundamentally, we are all dealt a hand of cards—ranging from our genes to the family and neighborhood we grew up in—which shapes how we adapt to these circumstances.

Personal alignment is how well we play that hand so that our decisions match our capabilities and aspirations. The game is complex and gradual. As children, our parents guide us, then ease away until we are virtually independent. We select a college and then a first job, often making choices without even beginning to know what we really don't know. We move on, reacting to opportunities, coping with disappointments. As we succeed, and especially as we fail, we mature and learn more and more about the consequences of our choices. The nature of the game and its choices change dramatically from age thirty to age forty-five to age sixty, yet the fundamentals remain largely constant. We must build on the hand of cards we're dealt and adapt to changing circumstances.

Achieving personal alignment requires the wisdom and discipline to understand and accept yourself and these enduring fundamentals. It requires asking—and answering—tough questions about your future: What do you want to accomplish, personally and professionally? As a professional, how do you want to allocate your time and efforts among your various roles? Beyond your career, what are your goals with respect to your family, your community, and yourself? What relationship are you seeking between your work and these other aspects of your life?

Engaging in such reflection is difficult and takes time and explicit attention. The process of personal alignment may begin with the commencement speaker who urges you to reflect on the advantages you've been given and how you will apply them in the years ahead. But if it stops there, you're in trouble because the challenge of leading a fulfilling life lies in consistent attention to your own priorities. It takes discipline to overcome the inertia generated by the daily demands of clients, colleagues, and the firm. To make conscious tradeoffs across life's dimensions ("I will take that vacation," "I will spend more time with my spouse"). To appreciate your own strengths and accept the limitations of your weaknesses. What distinguishes the men and women who succeed from those who fail is the efficacy of their actions, not the spaciousness of their hopes. If they believe their lives are out of alignment with their capabilities, goals, and needs, they make choices and take actions to correct the situation.

Success in a PSF is 10 percent strategy, 90 percent implementation. So, too, with individuals. Your actions, your daily behavior, are ultimately what matter most. Many executives want to become CEOs, for example, but only a few have the drive and dedication to actually *do* what is necessary. Unfortunately, many of us fail to follow through on our goals and decisions. We fail to make the necessary sacrifices and tradeoffs. Why is this?

Aligning a life, it turns out, is much more complex than aligning a business. A commercial enterprise is basically one-dimensional: It must win in the marketplace or perish. A business does not value life's journey, only its financial achievements. For human beings, the experience of the journey is an achievement all its own; we *live* lives filled with joys and sorrows, love and hate, pleasure and pain. If life were business, then our net worth would define happiness. Instead, we dream of living our finite years as fully as possible, across a variety of dimensions. As we age, our perspectives evolve; we develop different visions and goals for ourselves—accompanied by varying strategies, decisions, and behaviors. Sorting all this out is *not* easy.

Nevertheless, doing so is well worth the effort for you, *and* for your firm. Professionals who find fulfillment in life, who are essentially aligned around their personal goals, are more productive and motivated. They become better leaders as their enthusiasm and satisfaction invigorate their colleagues. They become starmakers, who better nurture and develop colleagues. Because their lives feel aligned, they see no need to search for greener pastures. In many ways, personal alignment is as valuable for the firm as it is for the individual.

We, Jay and Tom, don't claim to have the answers to life's questions. Far from it! But over the years, we've each made our share of mistakes and wrestled with our own conflicting goals. We've coached, collaborated, and consulted with hundreds of professionals, young and old, in a wide array of firms. Every individual's situation is unique, yet there are similarities. We all crave demanding, fulfilling careers. We want financial security, but not at the expense of other dimensions in our lives. We love our spouse and kids (and grandkids), and are forever trying to balance the demands of the office, with the joys and needs of home. We hope to contribute to our community, nurture friendships, and enjoy the spiritual camaraderie of church, mosque, or synagogue. We want to have fun, to learn, to give back. We yearn to live a valuable, fulfilling life and to leave a few footprints in the sand when our days are done.

Professionals: Different yet Similar

Whether you are a young professional striving to become a partner or an established leader in your firm, you are in an exceptionally demanding career. The intellectual and emotional challenges of your work are great, and the hours are long. Many weeks, there is little (if any) time for anything other than work and sleep. For younger readers, the goal of making it to partner or its equivalent may be compelling and make any amount of effort seem worthwhile. But as more experienced readers surely know, although the rewards of this accomplishment are great, the demands of the job don't diminish once you've arrived. On the contrary, the pace of work continues and even expands as the responsibilities of being an owner and a firm leader kick in.

To complicate matters further, highly successful professionals tend to share several characteristics, which contribute to their professional success but also tend to get in the way when they try to align the various aspects of their lives. Generalizing about a population as large and diverse as the readership of this book is always risky. Yet we suspect that at least some of the following description will resonate with many of you:

- You enjoy your craft. The intellectual challenges of your profession fascinate you, and you know that the stimulation and independence it provides would be hard to replicate elsewhere.

- Work is at the core of your life, setting your daily schedule and dictating your family and personal life, possibly more than you allow yourself to recognize.

- You greatly value your firm and your colleagues.

- You can become so absorbed by work that you ignore other issues in your life, including the tough questions about your future career and your aspirations.

If you—like the two of us—see aspects of yourself in this profile, it's probably worth pausing to reflect on where you've been, how you've achieved your success, and, most important, where you want to head. In other words, create your own sense of direction, your own personal strategy.

"You Are Here": The Power of Feedback

Basic business strategy requires companies to examine their circumstances with objective, even ruthless clarity. Understanding and accepting the critical facts about competitive position, relative cost and quality, customer loyalty, and market dynamics is the precursor to effective action. Developing your sense of personal direction requires the same kind of thoughtful attention. It requires appreciating where "Here" is across all the dimensions of your life. This means understanding the state of your family life as thoroughly as you do your client relationships. Reflecting on your spiritual life and your contributions to your community. Considering your personal friendships as well as your professional relationships. From career challenges, to health considerations, to family matters, you have to stare reality in the face. It isn't always a pretty picture.

And because it isn't pretty, it's tempting to turn away, go back to work, and hope for the best. The "best" isn't likely to happen, however, unless you make the effort to understand and accept the reality of your circumstances.

You might seek the perspectives of your friends, colleagues, and family members. How do they see you at present? What is their view of your strengths, and what would they like to see you do differently? What behaviors do they suggest that you stop? Start? Continue? You may not like what you hear, and you may not agree with it. Certainly you don't have to follow all (or any) of the advice you're given. However, our experience tells us that if you approach such dialogues with an open mind, you'll learn a lot about yourself. It will also prompt thinking about the past and how you may want to address the future. The tradeoffs and choices in your life will come into sharper focus. Heightened understanding can lead to better personal decisions.

Honest feedback is a valuable—albeit often painful—gift. Seeking it out is not a natural act. We all want to protect ourselves, to solicit only those perspectives that reinforce our positive self-image. To hear what we agree with, and discard the rest. We rationalize this behavior in a million different ways, from discrediting the source of a disagreeable perspective ("What do they really know?") to "accidentally" forgetting the feedback a few days later. That is why it takes conscious effort to see ourselves as others truly see us, rather than as we'd like to think they do.

Ironically, it is often much easier to get clarity professionally than personally. As we have seen, outstanding firms find ways to make constructive feedback an ongoing part of their professionals' lives. But performance reviews about your personal life are anything but routine and a lot tougher to facilitate. Nevertheless, try listening carefully to your spouse's concerns and understanding how you look through your children's eyes. Try keeping notes—perhaps even a journal. Gradually, seeking and accepting feedback will become a habit, a way of living. Like a captain at sea, you'll be able to plot your life's coordinates and accept the reality that, "I am here."

A Personal Point of Arrival

Like the captain, you'll also navigate life's seas more successfully if you have a point on the horizon toward which to steer. This means clarifying a point of arrival, being explicit about where you want your life to go on all of its dimensions—career and family, community and self. It also means reassessing this direction as your circumstances and life evolve.

A set of tough personal tradeoffs will likely be embedded in that point of arrival. Money offers a superb illustration. Most professionals, much of the time, behave as if more money is categorically better than less. Early on, they dream of a million-dollar net worth as their objective. Then that million dollars drifts to five million, perhaps even ten million. As careers progress, financial objectives inexorably ratchet upward. But should a professional strive to "maximize" her net worth? It all depends on you, and where you are headed.

Maximizing one of life's variables (such as net worth) usually comes at the direct expense of others (such as free time). More money is better only if the tradeoffs it requires don't undermine other dimensions of your desired point of arrival. Even the wealthiest among us agree that at some level, money has diminishing marginal returns. But since money is a common scorecard, it can gradually become an end in and of itself—with the consequence that more always seems better.

It is surprisingly rare for professionals to set explicit financial objectives and then behave differently once those objectives have been met: by working part-time, for instance, or by taking a lengthy sabbatical. Instead, old habits win out and we obsess over our net worth as the stock market gyrates. Many experienced professionals assert that they would gladly trade off 10 to 20 percent less income for 10 to 20 percent more personal time, yet they rarely behave that way. They go wherever client and firm demands carry them. And as the old saying goes, "If you don't know where you're going, any road will take you there."

Discovering your personal point of arrival means tackling the really tough questions head-on. What does *wealth* mean to you? How much is enough? How long do you want to pursue your career? Are there second or third careers in your future? When and how will you exit your firm? How will you feel if your children reach adulthood, and you haven't really gotten to know them—or they you? How serious are your spouse's escalating expressions of dissatisfaction with your relationship and time together? What does *success* mean to you? These are all hard questions, but the answers—and how you act on them—will surely be key to how you feel about yourself ten or twenty years from now.

In the introduction we referred to Einstein's observation that "Questions are more important than answers." That observation is even more crucial in this context. Without honest questions, there can be no useful answers. And even with the questions, the answers are never absolute. A new thirty-year-old partner with a young family and an enormous mortgage will likely answer the same questions differently than a fifty-something senior partner with ample net worth and grown children. But until you've explicitly defined your life's goals and aspirations, you can't really know what tradeoffs you're willing to make to reach them.

Life Strategies

A destination is incomplete without a map for the journey. Some professionals "wing it" and get lucky. Others allow themselves to be buffeted by circumstances. A thoughtful few begin to plan their life's strategy in their twenties and continue into their seventies. They understand that an effective personal strategy is more important than a business strategy—and much more complex.

Like a business strategy, a personal strategy emerges as a "stream of decisions made over time."[1] The central decisions almost always revolve around resource deployment, and the resources you have are your time and your energy. Achieving your point of arrival at any phase of your life is therefore highly dependent on your strategy for deploying these two assets.

Because your professional and financial performance turns on the effective utilization of your time, the dilemmas this creates are real and unavoidable. Explicitly or implicitly, you're selling your time to others: your clients and your firm. In fact, if the marketplace isn't buying your time (as a producer and/or manager), your career is probably headed downhill. Time and skill are a professional's only real product, and the incentive to sell as much of that product as possible to the highest bidder is great—even if that conflicts with your personal needs.

The phrase *life balance* barely begins to capture the subtleties of this conflict. How easily can a lawyer say "no" to an important client, even though the subsequent work will take him away from his family four nights a week? How does a consultant trade off her time between a boring large project and an exciting, but tiny, new client? You love your kids, but time at home will constrain your billable hours and revenue performance. Besides, the latter two will determine your income and that will help pay for the kids' education.

A wise man once asserted that each of us is defined by our commitments. Certainly that's true for professionals. You are defined by the clients you serve, and the clients you walk away from; by the assignments you accept, and those you reject. You are defined by the balance you strike between being a "producer" and a "manager," in tandem with the Little League games you do (or don't) attend. You are defined by the choices you make. Over time, those cumulative choices become your personal strategy and ultimately they will determine whether you realize your aspirations.

Therein lies an insight: *Do not* allow others to make personal choices for you. *Do not* unwittingly suppress your life's strategy to the incessant demands of others. *Do not* automatically go with the flow. Since time is your only currency, be deliberate and disciplined about its expenditure in the context of your goals. This will inevitably create conflicts among clients, firm, and family, since thoughtful choices require saying "yes" to some activities and "no" to others. Yet if you don't make explicit decisions and manage these conflicts, you can kiss your aspirations good-bye. You won't reach your destination if you allow others to map the route.

Develop Yourself

Implementing a personal strategy over decades, while developing yourself personally as well as professionally, makes pursuing a firm's competitive strategy look like a walk in the park. Fortunately, enough seasoned professionals have taken on the challenge to allow the rest of us to benefit from their experience. And while learning from your mistakes isn't what's usually called "best practice," in this arena that's the way most of the advice that follows has been learned.

First, aggressively manage your career. By exercising a strong, disciplined voice in how you spend your time—the clients you work with, the problems you tackle, the locations you work in—you will shape your portfolio of skills. Cumulatively, these experiences and skills will define your professional profile and amplify your desired personal "strategic identity."

Second, recognize that relationships, both internal and external, matter enormously. It's not the size of your Rolodex, but the level of mutual trust and respect you share with others that will ultimately help you achieve your goals. If clients and colleagues truly trust and respect you, they are more likely to accept the choices you make in allocating your time—even if they wish they could have more of it.

Third, take responsibility for your own learning. The fact that you may already be successful doesn't mean that you've achieved your full potential. Think of yourself as a work in progress, whatever your age. The world and your profession are constantly changing, and so can you. We've already spoken about the importance of feedback and the need to seek it out. Use what you learn to help you identify and build on your personal strengths, as well as to minimize and compensate for your limitations. You cannot be the "perfect" professional. Nobody can, so be realistic. Be yourself and build on your own capabilities. Lead from your strengths.

At the same time, there are some core competencies that all professionals need, which are essential to continually upgrade. Chief among them are the attributes of emotional intelligence that we described in chapter 8. You won't achieve your potential with clients or colleagues unless you can talk and *listen* to them effectively.

Beware strategic obsolescence. In a dynamic world, yesterday's skills must be continually upgraded to meet tomorrow's demands. Read, study, and think outside your traditional comfort zone. Pursue new types of projects with new colleagues.

Contrary to conventional wisdom, business turmoil may be your friend, allowing you to better demonstrate your capabilities and the value you add to your organization. During tumultuous times, businesses either lose share or gain share. The same is true for individuals. If you know your personal goals and you're clear-minded about your life strategy, then the turmoil created by a recession, or merger, or reorganization can be an opportunity for gaining personal advantage. It may prompt a "battlefield promotion" at your firm or cause you to pursue a fruitful new direction.

During such times, the ability to steer your life toward an explicit point on the horizon is more important than ever. If you understand what you really want for yourself, you're likely to find it easier to exercise leadership within the firm without becoming consumed by what may appear a no-win proposition. As a firm leader, you'll be able to do your best to sustain and build the firm on its new course. But you'll also be able to develop and remain open-minded to a personal "plan B," so that if things don't work out you'll know how and when to exit.

Finally, never stop leading from within your organization. Respect others, practice humility, and recognize the difference between self-confidence and egotism. When you're working with colleagues and clients, remember that life has lots of ups and downs, and that all of us shuttle in and out of the winner's circle at various times. Others will be able to tell whether or not you genuinely want to help them succeed. In fact, the more you lead from within, the more influence you'll have and the better able you'll be to achieve your goals and aspirations.

The Evolving You

Personal life goals naturally evolve as circumstances change. As John Gardner observed in *Self-Renewal*, "Most of us have potentialities that have never been developed simply because the circumstances of our lives never called them forth."[2] A promotion, a new child, a divorce, or a death in the family can be the opportunity to seriously rethink your point of arrival. Fundamental changes—some anticipated and some unanticipated—shape everyone's destiny. The challenge is to turn them to your advantage, to use them as opportunities for self-renewal.

From time to time, everyone benefits from being "re-potted," from applying their talents to new challenges. Re-potting and self-renewal go hand in hand, whether the pot is a new position, a new firm, or an entirely new career. Re-potting always feels risky at first, since you're trading the comfort of familiar experience for uncertainty. But the greater risk is to remain imprisoned in an old pot you have long since outgrown. In a new environment, you can grow to meet new challenges with new energy; in the old one, you run the risk of atrophy.

At some point, you may decide to leave your firm for a "better" opportunity. Be courageous but proceed with caution. You have lots of data about your own organization; you understand the limitations and weaknesses of your personal circumstances. In contrast, you can only evaluate the veneer of other opportunities—especially when the recruiters are in sell mode. Far too many professionals leap at enticing new jobs only to discover that they are worse off than before.

Re-potting is valuable if it takes place in the context of your aspirations, your point of arrival. People succeed when they run toward something rather than away from something.

The same principle applies to retirement strategies. Simply telling yourself to "wait and see" may seem comforting, but as a strategy it's deeply flawed because, again, you're allowing circumstances to drive your life, rather than vice versa. The further you are from retirement, the harder it will be to engage. Nevertheless, start thinking about it now, lest you discover that delay is indeed the deadliest form of denial. What are the rules or cultural norms in your firm and profession? There is immense variation: Goldman Sachs expects its partners to leave in their fifties. Historically, they were made limited partners, and usually pursued careers working for nonprofits or the government. At the other extreme, many law firms permit their partners to continue their legal work by being "of counsel" as long as they are interested and able.

Whatever your firm's particular practices, the important question is, "What is right for you, and how will you pursue it?" One size does not fit all. Each individual has to find the unique solutions that feel right for her or him at that phase of life.

Build a Life, Not a Resume

Whether you know it or not, you may have a challenge looming ahead. An increasingly fundamental challenge that you may artfully ignore. One you stare at in the mirror every morning. That challenge is you.

If you are like many of the professionals we know, you're a superbly trained "type A" overachiever. As a schoolchild, your single-minded competitiveness yielded outstanding report cards, which in turn "promoted" you to top-tier academic opportunities. University and professional school further honed these instincts. When you entered the work world (typically at an early age), you were a ladder climber par excellence. And climb you did. Promotion to partner (or the equivalent) offered a glorious opportunity to celebrate your achievements—a euphoria that lasted at least a few weeks until you realized that you were now perched on the bottom rung of a significantly more demanding ladder.

Now, when you glance in the mirror, you see an accomplished professional. The challenge—and it's a big one—is to see the other dimensions of your life in equally bright light. Can you remember the dreams of your youth, when life felt more like an extraordinary adventure?

Somewhere while climbing the ladder, you may have lost sight of the larger picture. Working weekends became an ingrained habit, just like bringing your cell phone to soccer games, or flying home early from the family vacation. You recall a professor who once claimed that life could be organized into phases where a person first learns, then earns, and finally serves. You rationalize your behavior: You're in the earning phase of your life—even if you've been in that same phase for decades!

Perhaps so. But have your habits changed? Or as your life moves on, do you still have a twenty-eight-year-old's schedule loaded into a forty-eight-year-old's PalmPilot?

More important, are you putting aspects of your life partially on hold while you ascend from rung to rung? Are there voices calling from the ground below your ladder—voices of children, a spouse, or a close friend? Voices calling you to public service or toward a radically new career? Your time has no shelf life. Today's sacrifices and tradeoffs cannot be recouped tomorrow.

A basic rule of nature exacerbates this problem for most of us. Behavior is incremental; we live our lives hour by hour, day by day. It doesn't really matter if you miss a single piano recital or a week of exercise. But if it becomes a habit, then a year later it may matter a lot. It's the *cumulative* effect of our behavior (and the tradeoffs we make) that generate significant consequences. In the financial world, this phenomenon is often referred to as the "magic of compounding." Invest a dollar for twenty years at 5 percent interest, and you get $2.65 two decades later. Increase the rate to 10 percent, and you earn $6.73. While the interest rate doubles, the returns triple. Behavior, for better and worse, compounds over time like money, yielding high personal returns in some areas and disasters in others. And since we have only a fixed amount of currency (our time) to invest, we cannot possibly invest everywhere. We *decide* what opportunities (like exercise or the piano recital) to pass up.

You control your destiny; no one is dictating your personal tradeoffs and decisions. Sure, there are always short-term constraints. But over the next few years you also have enormous degrees of personal freedom. Especially in a world in which multiple careers, part-time work, and telecommuting are increasingly the norm. Your life has phases that can provide varying challenges and opportunities—if you choose to recognize them. Building an impressive resume is a lot easier than building a fulfilling life because life is a lot more complicated. It's not a ladder at all, but rather a continuum with confusing twists and turns. Being smart helps; being wise, thoughtful, and disciplined is an absolute necessity.

We've seen stars succeed at life, and we've seen stars fail life miserably, despite professional success. Those that succeed build lives as well as resumes. When they stare in the mirror, they don't see just a professional; they see a parent, a spouse, a friend, and a member of the community. They assess their progress objectively against a broad multidimensional scorecard, on which their resume is only one of the indicators. They are never fully aligned, but always aligning. They struggle, fail, and succeed; then they struggle some more.

Sometimes they are afraid, because some of their life decisions cut against conventional wisdom or current inertia. Then confidence returns and assures them that the risk is not as great as it feels. In the end, it is not the risk of failure, but rather the risk of not trying that matters most.

These men and women are a star's star, starmakers and their firm's most precious asset. Their client relationships generate the revenue that pays the bills and the bonuses. Their leadership behavior shapes the destiny of their firm and the impact of its strategy.

Their aspirations and values motivate others: families and friends, colleagues and clients. They are doing their best to build outstanding lives given their personal circumstances.

What about *you?*

Appendix: Firms Represented in the Study

Accounting

Ernst & Young LLP
Price Waterhouse LLP (now PricewaterhouseCoopers)

Advertising

Grey Advertising, Inc. (now Grey Worldwide)
Ogilvy & Mather
Young & Rubicam, Inc.

Executive Search

Heidrick & Struggles International, Inc.
Korn/Ferry International

Investment Banks

Alex. Brown Incorporated (now Deutsche Banc Alex. Brown)
Goldman Sachs (now The Goldman Sachs Group, Inc.)
Hambrecht & Quist LLC (now J. P. Morgan H&Q)

IT Consulting

American Management Systems, Inc.

IBM Consulting (now IBM Global Services)

Law

Fulbright & Jaworski LLP

Latham & Watkins

Skadden, Arps, Slate, Meagher & Flom LLP

Wachtell, Lipton, Rosen & Katz

Management Consulting

Bain & Company, Inc.

McKinsey & Company, Inc.

Notes

Chapter 1

1. *Alignment* was first introduced into the lexicon of organization and management in the 1960s by a group of organization scholars including Jay Lorsch and his colleague, Paul Lawrence (*Organization and Environment* [Boston: Harvard Business School Press, 1967]). It was introduced to a broader management audience in 1982 by Thomas J. Peters and Robert H. Waterman, Jr., in *In Search of Excellence: Lessons from America's Best-Run Companies* (New York: Harper & Row, 1982).

Chapter 2

1. Compiled from the following sources: IDC "Worldwide Consulting Forecasts," 1995–2002, 1997–2004; Kennedy Information Group; Securities Data Corporation database; *The American Lawyer*; *Advertising Age*; *Accounting Today*; U.S. Industry and Trade Outlook; Business Insurance; U.S. Market Trends & Forecasts; Euromonitor; Salomon Smith Barney; "Economic Indicators," Council of Economic Advisors, United States Government, January 2001 and March 1995; Statistical Abstract of the United States, United States Government, 2000; "Flow of Funds Accounts of the United States: Annual Flows and Outstandings 1995–2000," Board of Governors of the Federal Reserve System, 9 March 2001.

2. Maister, David H., *Managing the Professional Service Firm* (New York: Free Press, 1993).

3. Dun and Bradstreet; Association of American Publishers, "Preliminary Estimated Book Publishing Industry Net Sales, 1992, 1997–2000."

4. Peter Drucker, quoted in Peter Schwartz, "Post Capitalist," *WIRED* magazine, July/August 1993.

5. John H. Kennedy, "Death of a Law Firm," *Boston Globe*, 10 November 1991, p. A37.

6. Compiled from the following sources: "PwC's Law Network Expands in Hungary," *International Accounting Bulletin*, 30 June 2000; Denise Collins, "Korn/Ferry's Futurestep and the *Wall Street Journal* Team Up to Revolutionize Executive Search and Recruitment Advertising," *Business Wire*, 8 June 1998; McKinsey & Company Web site, <www.McKinsey.com>: "The Business Technology Office (a.k.a. "BTO") is a virtual office operating as one global office. Its consultants reside in several geographic locations"; Jennifer Hagendorf, "Dot-Com Dozen: Looking toward Next Generation—IBM Global Services Hones Internet Start-Up Offerings," *Computer Reseller News*, 17 April 2000; "AMS Forms International Financial Portal," *The Financial News*, 28 August 2000; WPP Web site: <www.wpp.com>; "Business Brief— General Motors Corp.: EDS Buys A.T. Kearney in $300 Million Transaction," *Wall Street Journal*, 5 September 1995; David Cho, "Cisco Sinks $1 B into KPMG Consulting," *Accounting Today*, 23 August 1999.

7. D&B Desktop Solutions for Windows, 2001 data. Copyright 1998 Dun & Bradstreet. Onesource Information Systems, 2001.

8. Compiled from the following sources: Richard Siklos, "Accounting Mega Merger: Coopers & Lybrand and Price Waterhouse plan to merge, a move that will catapult the new entity into top slot among the world's accounting and consulting firms," *The Financial Post*, 19 September 1997; Kevin McQuaid, "A Titan Grows in Gotham; Acquisition: In acquiring Alex Brown, Bankers Trust is gaining a quality subsidiary and positioning itself to offer a wider array of financial products," *Baltimore Sun*, 13 April 1997; Emerson's Professional Service Review, "Cap Gemini Ernst & Young finally to complete acquisition" (Bellevue: The Emerson Companies), 1 January 2001; "Rogers & Wells, UK law firm Clifford Chance agree to merge," Associated Press Newswires, 12 July 1999; Morgan Stanley Dean Witter analyst report, "Korn/Ferry International," 27 February 2001; Sinclair Stewart, "Interpublic Gobbles Up True North: US$2.1B Takeover: Union of Rivals Creates World's Largest Ad Company," *Financial Post*, 20 March 2001; "Publicis Closes Buy of Saatchi & Saatchi," Dow Jones News Service, 11 September 2000; Credit Suisse First Boston analyst report, "WPP Group," 26 February 2001; Securities Data Corporation.

9. Compiled from the following sources: National Association for Law Placement, comparison of 1999 and 2000 salary surveys (Washington, DC: National Association for Law Placement); "Class of 2000 Career Data," Harvard Business School MBA Career Services Web site, <www.hbs.edu/admin/>; "Facts, Figures, and Frequently Asked Questions," Stanford Business School Web site, <www.stanford.edu/home/stanford/facts/>; and "Placement Overview," Wharton School Web site, <www.wharton.upenn.edu/>.

10. Debora Vrana, "The Cutting Edge: California Dealin'—Executive Recruiter Korn/Ferry to Launch Long-Delayed IPO," *Los Angeles Times*, 8 February 1999, C1.

11. Linklaters & Alliance and "The Way We Were, 1990–1999," *The American Lawyer*, 5 July 2000.

12. Information compiled from: USB Warburg analyst report, "Riding the Internet HR Wave," 25 July 2000; "Earnie—Four Years of Online Consulting," *Journal of Management Consulting*, 1 May 2000; Funds International, "Goldman Sachs to Beef Up Web Presence," 29 August 2000; David Futrelle, "What a Million Bucks Buys: Sites for the Wealthy Have Slightly Better Tools and Much Higher Prices," *Money*, 1 February 2001.

13. Chris Zook and James Allen, *Profit from the Core: Growth Strategy in an Era of Turbulence* (Boston: Harvard Business School Press, 2001).

Chapter 3

1. Kenneth R. Andrews, *The Concept of Corporate Strategy*, revised ed. (Homewood, IL: Richard D. Irwin, 1980), 18.

2. "CN50: The World's Largest Consulting Firms," *Consultant News* 31, no. 6 (June 2001): 6–7.

3. Chris Zook and James Allen, *Profit from the Core: Growth Strategy in an Era of Turbulence* (Boston: Harvard Business School Press, 2001).

4. James C. Collins and Jerry I. Porras, *Built to Last: Successful Habits of Visionary Companies* (New York: HarperCollins, 1994), 17–18.

5. Both Hambrecht & Quist and Alex Brown have undergone ownership transitions since we began studying them. H&Q is now part of Chase (in December 1999), and Alex Brown was sold to Bankers Trust (in September 1997), which was subsequently purchased by Deutsche Bank (in June 1999). Over time, these changes are likely to have a marked influence on the firms' internal and external strategic identities.

Chapter 7

1. Joseph Kahn, "Plan to Go Public at Goldman, Sachs," *New York Times*, 15 June 1998, A1.

2. Thomas Stewart, "The House That Knowledge Built," *Fortune*, 2 October 2000, 278.

3. Herminia Ibarra and Nicol Sakley, "Charlotte Beers at Ogilvy & Mather Worldwide (A)," Case 9-495-031 (Boston: Harvard Business School, 1999).

Chapter 8

1. Amar Bhide, "McKinsey & Company (A): 1956," Case 9-393-066 (Boston: Harvard Business School, 1992).

2. Daniel Goleman, "What Makes a Leader," *Harvard Business Review* 76, no. 6 (November–December, 1998). Also, Daniel Goleman, *Emotional Intelligence: Why It Can Matter More Than IQ, for Character, Health, and Lifelong Achievement* (New York: Bantam, 1998).

3. Jim Collins presents a similar portrait of highly effective corporate leaders in "Level 5 Leadership: The Triumph of Humility and Fierce Resolve," *Harvard Business Review* 79, no. 1 (January 2001).

4. Herminia Ibarra and Nicol Sakley, "Charlotte Beers at Ogilvy & Mather Worldwide (A)," Case 9-495-031 (Boston: Harvard Business School, 1999).

5. Frederick F. Reichheld, *The Loyalty Effect* (Boston: Harvard Business School Press, 1996).

Chapter 9

1. Kenneth R. Andrews, *The Concept of Corporate Strategy*, revised ed. (Homewood, IL: Richard D. Irwin, 1980), 18.

2. John W. Gardner, *Self-Renewal: The Individual and the Innovative Society*, paperback reissue edition (New York: W.W. Norton, 1995), 11.

Index

About the Authors

Jay W. Lorsch is the Louis E. Kirstein Professor of Human Relations at the Harvard Business School. He is the Cofounder and Chair of the School's Executive Education program, Leading Professional Service Firms, which is the only university-based program focusing on the leadership and management of such firms. His interest in professional service firms began in 1987 when he coauthored the *Harvard Business Review* article "When Professionals Have to Manage." His interest also grew as a result of his leadership positions at HBS where he was a Senior Associate Dean from 1986 to 1995, responsible first for the faculty's research activities and later for its Executive Education programs. In these positions he gained firsthand experience in leading professionals.

He is the author of numerous articles and fifteen books, including *Organization and Environment*, which won the Academy of Management Book Award and the James A. Hamilton Hospital Administration Book Award, and *Pawns or Potentates: The Reality of America's Corporate Boards*. He has also served as a consultant to many professional service firms, including Coopers & Lybrand, Goldman Sachs, McGuire Woods Battle & Boothe, Morgan Stanley, and Watson Wyatt.

Professor Lorsch has taught thousands of M.B.A. and Executive Education students at HBS. Of most relevance to *Aligning the Stars* are the almost 2,000 leaders of professional service firms from around the world who have participated in Leading Professional Service Firms. Their problems, questions, and discussions were the initial stimulus for the research that led to this book.

Jay and his wife, Patricia, live in Cambridge, Massachusetts, and have five adult children.

Thomas J. Tierney is a Director and the former Chief Executive of Bain & Company, where he served in many capacities for over two decades. As CEO, he helped lead Bain's resurgence following a management buy-out from its founders in 1991. During the 1990s, the strategy consulting firm increased revenue sixfold, and expanded from twelve to twenty-six offices worldwide. Bain has been widely recognized for its ability to attract, retain, and motivate star talent.

Complementing his hands-on experience, Tierney has consulted with professional service firms on issues of competitive strategy, growth, and organizational effectiveness. He has lectured at Harvard Business School and taught in Harvard's Executive Education program for professional firm leaders. His emphasis on teaching led to his inclusion in the book *Learning from the CEO*.

In 2000, Tierney stepped down as Chief Executive to pursue a deeply felt passion: improving the practice of management in the nonprofit sector. To this end, he founded The Bridgespan Group, an independent nonprofit affiliate of Bain & Company, which provides consulting services to nonprofit organizations and foundations. He serves as Chairman of this endeavor, in addition to his active involvement with a variety of related boards and initiatives.

A graduate of U.C. Davis and Harvard Business School, Mr. Tierney lives in the Boston area with his wife, Karen, and their sons, Colin and Braden.